Introduction to the Philosophy of History

GEORG HEGEL

Printed in Scotts Valley, CA - USA.

Hegel, Georg.

Introduction to the Philosophy of History / Georg Hegel – 1st ed.

1. History 2. Philosophy

TABLE OF CONTENTS

Translator's Introduction

Hegel's Lectures on the Philosophy of History are recognized in Germany as a popular introduction to his system; their form is less rigid than the generality of metaphysical treatises, and the illustrations, which occupy a large proportion of the work, are drawn from a field of observation more familiar perhaps, than any other, to those who have not devoted much time to metaphysical studies. One great value of the work is that it presents the leading facts of history from an altogether novel point of view. And when it is considered that the writings of Hegel have exercised a marked influence on the political movements of Germany, it will be admitted that his theory of the universe, especially that part which bears directly upon politics, deserves attention even from those who are the most exclusive advocates of the "practical."

A writer who has established his claim to be regarded as an authority, by the life which he has infused into metaphysical abstractions, has pronounced the work before us, "one of the pleasantest books on the subject he ever read."[1]

And compared with that of most German writers, even the style may claim to be called vigorous and pointed. If therefore in its English dress the "Philosophy of History" should be found deficient in this respect, the fault must not be attributed to the original.

It has been the aim of the translator to present his author to the public in a really English form, even at the cost of a circumlocution which must sometimes do injustice to the merits of the original. A few words however have necessarily been used in a rather unusual sense; and one of them is of very frequent occurrence. The German "Geist," in Hegel's nomenclature, includes both intelligence and will, the latter even more expressly than the former. It embraces in fact man's entire mental and moral being, and a little reflection will make it obvious that no term in our metaphysical vocabulary could have been well substituted for the more theological one, "Spirit," as a fair equivalent. It is indeed only the impersonal and abstract use of the term that is open to objection; an

5

objection which can be met by an appeal to the best classical usage; viz., the rendering of the Hebrew; and Greek pneuma in the authorized version of the Scriptures. One indisputable instance may suffice in confirmation: "Their horses [*i.e.*, of the Egyptians] are flesh and not *spirit*." (Isaiah xxxi. 3.) It is pertinent to remark here, that the comparative disuse of this term in English metaphysical literature, is one result of that alienation of theology from philosophy with which continental writers of the most opposite schools agree in taxing the speculative genius of Britain – an alienation which mainly accounts for the gulf separating English from German speculation, and which will, it is feared, on other accounts also be the occasion of communicating a somewhat uninviting aspect to the following pages.

The distinction which the Germans make between "Sittlichkeit" and "Moralität," has presented another difficulty. The former denotes conventional morality, the latter that of the heart or conscience. Where no ambiguity was likely to arise, both terms have been translated "morality." In other cases a stricter rendering has been given, modified by the requirements of the context. The word "moment" is, as readers of German philosophy are aware, a veritable crux to the translator. In Mr. J. R. Morell's very valuable edition of Johnson's Translation of Tennemann's "Manual of the History of Philosophy," the following explanation is given: "This term was borrowed from mechanics by Hegel (see his "Wissenschaft der Logik," Vol. 3, P. 104, Ed. 1841). He employs it to denote the contending forces which are mutually dependent, and whose contradiction forms an equation. Hence his formula, *Esse* = Nothing. Here *Esse* and Nothing are momentums, giving birth to *Werden, i.e.,* Existence. Thus the momentum contributes to the same oneness of operation in contradictory forces that we see in mechanics, amidst contrast and diversity, in weight and distance, in the case of the balance." But in several parts of the work before us this definition is not strictly adhered to, and the translator believes he has done justice to the original in rendering the word by "successive" or "organic phase." In the chapter on the Crusades another term occurs which could not be simply rendered into English. The definite, positive, and present embodiment of essential being is there spoken of as "ein *Dieses*," "das *Dieses*," etc., literally "a *This*," "the *This*," for which repulsive combination a periphrasis has been substituted, which, it is believed, is not only accurate but expository. Paraphrastic *additions,* however, have been, in fairness to the reader, enclosed in brackets []; and the philosophical appropriation of ordinary terms is generally indicated by capitals, *e.g.,* "Spirit," "Freedom," "State," "Nature," etc.

The limits of a brief preface preclude an attempt to explain the Hegelian method in its wider applications; and such an undertaking is rendered altogether unnecessary by the facilities which are afforded by works so very accessible as the translation of Tennemann above mentioned, Chalybseus's "Historical Development of Speculative Philosophy, from Kant to Hegel," Blakey's "History of the Philosophy of Mind," Mr. Lewes's "Biographical History of Philosophy," besides treatises devoted more particularly to the Hegelian philosophy. Among these latter may be fairly mentioned the work of a French professor, M. Vera, "Introduction à la Philosophie de Hegel," a lucid and earnest exposition of the system at large; and the very able summary of Hegel's "Philosophy of Right," by T. C. Sandars, late fellow of Oriel College, which forms one of the series of "Oxford Essays" for 1855, and which bears directly on the subject of the present volume.

It may, nevertheless, be of some service to the reader to indicate the point of view from which this "Philosophy of History" is composed, and to explain the leading idea. The aim and scope of that civilizing process which all hopeful thinkers recognize in history, is the attainment of Rational Freedom. But the very term freedom supposes a previous bondage; and the question naturally arises: "Bondage to what?" – A superficial inquirer may be satisfied with an answer referring it to the *physical power* of the ruling body. Such a response was deemed satisfactory by a large number of political speculators in the last century, and even at the beginning of the present; and it is one of the great merits of an influential thinker of our days to have expelled this *idolum fori,* which had also become an *idolum theatri,* from its undue position; and to have revived the simple truth that all stable organizations of men, all religious and political communities, are based upon principles which are far beyond the control of the One or the Many. And in these principles or some phase of them every man in every clime and age is born, lives and moves. The only question is: Whence are those principles derived?

Whence spring those primary beliefs or superstitions, religious and political, that hold society together? They are no inventions of "priestcraft" or "kingcraft," for to them priestcraft and kingcraft owe their power. They are no results of a *Contrat Social,* for with them society originates. Nor are they the mere suggestions of man's weakness, prompting him to propitiate the powers of nature, in furtherance of his finite, earthborn desires. Some of the phenomena of the religious systems that have prevailed in the world might seem thus explicable; but the Nihilism of more than one Oriental creed, the suicidal strivings of the Hindoo devotee to become absorbed in a divinity recognized as a pure negation, cannot be reduced to so gross a formula; while the political superstition that ascribes a divine right to the feebleness of a woman or an infant is altogether untouched by it. Nothing is left therefore but to recognize them as "fancies," "delusions," "dreams," the results of man's vain imagination – to class them with the other absurdities with which the abortive past of humanity is by some thought to be only too replete; or, on the other hand, to regard them as the rudimentary teachings of that essential intelligence in which man's intellectual and moral life originates. With Hegel they are the objective manifestation of infinite reason – the first promptings of Him who having "made of one blood all nations of men for to dwell on the face of the earth, hath determined *the times before appointed,* and the bounds of their habitation, if haply they might feel after and find him" – του γαρ και γενοσ εσμεν And it is these καιτοι προτεταγμενοι, these determined and organic epochs in the history of the world that Hegel proposes to distinguish and develop in the following treatise. Whatever view may be entertained as to the origin or importance of those elementary principles, and by whatever general name they may be called – Spontaneous, Primary, or Objective Intelligence – it seems demonstrable that it is in some sense or other to its *own* belief, its *own* reason or essential being, that imperfect humanity is in bondage; while the perfection of social existence is commonly regarded as a deliverance from that bondage. In the Hegelian system, this paradoxical condition is regarded as one phase of that antithesis which is presented in all spheres of existence, between the subjective and the objective, but which it is the result of the natural and intellectual processes that constitute the life of the universe, to annul by merging

8

into one absolute existence. And however startling this theory may be as applied to other departments of nature and intelligence, it appears to be no unreasonable formula for the course of civilization, and which is substantially as follows: In less cultivated nations, political and moral restrictions are looked upon as objectively posited; the constitution of society, like the world of natural objects, is regarded as something into which a man is inevitably born; and the individual feels himself bound to comply with requirements of whose justice or propriety he is not allowed to judge, though they often severely test his endurance, and even demand the sacrifice of his life. In a state of high civilization, on the contrary, though an equal self-sacrifice be called for, it is in respect of laws and institutions which are felt to be just and desirable. This change of relation may, without any very extraordinary use of terms, or extravagance of speculative conceit, be designated the harmonization or reconciliation of objective and subjective intelligence. The successive phases which humanity has assumed in passing from that primitive state of bondage to this condition of rational freedom form the chief subject of the following lectures.

The mental and moral condition of individuals and their social and religious conditions (the subjective and objective manifestations of reason) exhibit a strict correspondence with each other in every grade of progress. "They that make them are like unto them," is as true of religious and political ideas as of religious and political idols. Where man sets no value on that part of his mental and moral life which makes him superior to the brutes, brute life will be an object of worship and bestial sensuality will be the genius of the ritual. Where mere inaction is the *finis bonorum,* absorption in nothingness will be the aim of the devotee. Where, on the contrary, active and vigorous virtue is recognized as constituting the real value of man – where subjective spirit has learned to assert its own freedom, both against irrational and unjust requirements from without, and caprice, passion, and sensuality, from within, it will demand a living, acting, just, and holy, embodiment of Deity as the only possible object of its adoration. In the same degree, political principles also will be affected. Where mere nature predominates, no legal relations will be acknowledged but those based on natural distinction; rights will be inexorably associated with "caste."

9

Where, on the other hand, spirit has attained its freedom, it will require a code of laws and political constitution, in which the rational subordination of nature to reason that prevails in its own being, and the strength it feels to resist sensual seductions shall be distinctly mirrored.

Between the lowest and highest grades of intelligence and will, there are several intervening stages, around which a complex of derivative ideas, and of institutions, arts, and sciences, in harmony with them, are aggregated. Each of these aggregates has acquired a name in history as a distinct nationality. Where the distinctive principle is losing its vigor, as the result of the expansive force of mind of which it was only the temporary embodiment, the national life declines, and we have the transition to a higher grade, in which a comparatively abstract and limited phase of subjective intelligence and will – to which corresponds an equally imperfect phase of objective reason – is exchanged for one more concrete, and vigorous – one which develops human capabilities more freely and fully, and in which right is more adequately comprehended.

The goal of this contention is, as already indicated, the self-realization, the complete development of spirit, whose proper nature is freedom – freedom in both senses of the term, *i.e.* liberation from *outward* control – inasmuch as the law to which it submits has its own explicit sanction – and emancipation from the *inward* slavery of lust and passion.

The above remarks are not designed to afford anything like a complete or systematic analysis of Hegel's "Philosophy of History," but simply to indicate its leading conception, and if possible to contribute something towards removing a prejudice against it on the score of its resolving facts into mystical paradoxes, or attempting to construe them *à priori*. In applying the theory, some facts may not improbably have been distorted, some brought into undue prominence, and others altogether neglected. In the most cautious and limited analysis of the past, failures and perversions of this kind are inevitable: and a comprehensive view of history is proportionately open to mistake. But it is another question whether the principles applied in this work to explain the course which civilization has followed, are a correct inference from historical facts, and afford a reliable clue to the explanation of their leading aspects. The translator would remark, in conclusion, that the "Introduction" will probably be found the most tedious and difficult part of the treatise; he would therefore suggest a cursory reading of it in the first instance, and a second perusal as a *resume* of principles which are more completely illustrated in the body of the work.

J. Sibree.

CHARLES HEGEL'S PREFACE

The changed form in which Hegel's lectures on the Philosophy of History are re-issued, suggests the necessity of some explanation respecting the relation of this second edition both to the original materials from which the work was compiled, and to their first publication.

The lamented Professor Gans, the editor of the "Philosophy of History," displayed a talented ingenuity in transforming lectures into a book; in doing so he followed for the most part Hegel's latest deliveries of the course, because they were the most popular, and appeared most adapted to his object. He succeeded in presenting the lectures much as they were delivered in the winter of 1830-31; and this result might be regarded as perfectly satisfactory, if Hegel's various readings of the course had been more uniform and concordant, if indeed they had not rather been of such a nature as to supplement each other. For however great may have been Hegel's power of condensing the wide extent of the phenomenal world by thought, it was impossible for him entirely to master and to present in a uniform shape the immeasurable material of history in the course of one semester. In the first delivery in the winter of 1822-23, he was chiefly occupied with unfolding the philosophical idea, and showing how this constitutes the real kernel of history, and the impelling soul of world-historical peoples. In proceeding to treat of China and India, he wished, as he said himself, only to show by example how philosophy ought to comprehend the character of a nation; and this could be done more easily in the case of the stationary nations of the East, than in that of peoples which have a *bona, fide* history and a historical development of character. A warm predilection made him linger long with the Greeks, for whom he always felt a youthful enthusiasm; and after a brief consideration of the Roman World he endeavored finally to condense the Mediaeval Period and the Modern Time into a few lectures; for time pressed, and when, as in the Christian World, the thought no longer lies concealed among the multitude of phenomena, but announces itself and is obviously present in history, the philosopher is at liberty to abridge his discussion of it; in fact, nothing more is needed than to indicate the impelling idea. In the later readings, on the other hand, China, India, and the East generally were more speedily despatched, and more time and attention devoted to the German World. By degrees the philosophical and abstract occupied less space, the historical matter was expanded, and the whole became more popular. It is easy to see how the different readings of the course supplement each other, and how the entire substance cannot be gathered without uniting the philosophical element which predominates in the earlier, and which must constitute the basis of the work, with the historical expansion which characterizes the latest deliveries.

Had Hegel pursued the plan which most professors adopt, in adapting notes for use in the lecture room, of merely appending emendations and additions to the original draught, it would be correct to suppose that his latest readings would be also the most matured. But as, on the contrary, every delivery was with him a new act of thought, each gives only the expression of that degree of philosophical energy which animates his mind at the time; thus, in fact, the two first deliveries of 1822-23 and 1824-25, exhibit a far more comprehensive vigor of idea and expression, a far richer store of striking thoughts and appropriate images, than those of later date; for that first inspiration which accompanied the thoughts when they first sprang into existence, could only lose its living freshness by repetition.

From what has been said, the nature of the task which a new edition involved is sufficiently manifest. A treasury of thought of no trifling value had to be recovered from the first readings, and the tone of originality restored to the whole. The printed text therefore was made the basis, and the work of inserting, supplementing, substituting, and transforming (as the case seemed to require), was undertaken with the greatest possible respect for the original. No scope was left for the individual views of the editor, since in all such alterations Hegel's manuscripts were the sole guide. For while the first publication of these lectures – a part of the introduction excepted – followed the notes of the hearers only, the second edition has endeavored to supplement it by making Hegel's own manuscripts the basis throughout, and using the notes only for the purpose of rectification and arrangement. The editor

13

has striven after uniformity of tone through the whole work simply by allowing the author to speak everywhere in his own words; so that not only are the new insertions taken verbatim from the manuscripts, but even where the printed text was retained in the main, peculiar expressions which the hearer had lost in transcription, were restored.

For the benefit of those who place vigor of thought in a formal schematism, and with polemical zeal assert its exclusive claim against other styles of philosophizing, the remark may be added that Hegel adhered so little to the subdivisions which he had adopted, that he made some alterations in them on occasion of every reading of the course – treated Buddhism and Lamaism, *e.g.,* sometimes before, sometimes after India, sometimes reduced the Christian World more closely to the German nations, sometimes took in the Byzantine Empire, and so on. The new edition has had but few alterations to make in this respect. When the association for publishing Hegel's works did me the honor to intrust me with the re-editing of my father's "Philosophy of History," it also named as advocates of the claims of the first edition, and as representatives of Professor Gans, who had been removed from its circle by death, three of its members, Geh. Ober-Regierungs Rath Dr. Schulze, Professor von Henning, and Professor Hotho, to whose revision the work in its new shape was to be submitted. In this revision, I not only enjoyed the acquiescence of those most estimable men and valued friends in the alterations I had made, but also owe them a debt of thanks for many new emendations, which I take the opportunity of thus publicly discharging.

In conclusion, I feel constrained to acknowledge that my gratitude to that highly respected association for the praiseworthy deed of love to science, friendship, and disinterestedness, whose prosecution originated it and still holds it together, could be increased only by the fact of its having granted me also a share in editing the works of my beloved father.

Charles Hegel.

Introduction to the Philosophy of History

The subject of this course of Lectures is the Philosophical History of the World. And by this must be understood, not a collection of general observations respecting it, suggested by the study of its records, and proposed to be illustrated by its facts, but Universal History itself.[2] To gain a clear idea, at the outset, of the nature of our task, it seems necessary to begin with an examination of the other methods of treating History. The various methods may be ranged under three heads:

I.   Original History.

II.   Reflective History.

III.   Philosophical History.

I. Of the first kind, the mention of one or two distinguished names will furnish a definite type. To this category belong *Herodotus, Thucydides,* and other historians of the same order, whose descriptions are for the most part limited to deeds, events, and states of society, which they had before their eyes, and whose spirit they shared. They simply transferred what was passing in the world around them, to the realm of representative intellect. An external phenomenon is thus translated into an internal conception. In the same way the *poet* operates upon the material supplied him by his emotions; projecting it into an image for the conceptive faculty. These original historians did, it is true, find statements and narratives of other men ready to hand. One person cannot be an eye or ear witness of everything. But they make use of such aids only as the poet does of that heritage of an already-formed language, to which he owes so much: merely as an ingredient. Historiographers bind together the fleeting elements of story, and treasure them up for immortality in the Temple of Mnemosyne. Legends, Balladstories, Traditions, must be excluded from such original history. These are but dim and hazy forms of historical apprehension, and

15

therefore belong to nations whose intelligence is but half awakened. Here, on the contrary, we have to do with people fully conscious of what they were and what they were about. The domain of reality – actually seen, or capable of being so – affords a very different basis in point of firmness from that fugitive and shadowy element, in which were engendered those legends and poetic dreams whose historical prestige vanishes, as soon as nations have attained a mature individuality.

Such original historians, then, change the events, the deeds, and the states of society with which they are conversant, into an object for the conceptive faculty. The narratives they leave us cannot, therefore, be very comprehensive in their range. Herodotus, Thucydides, Guicciardini, may be taken as fair samples of the class in this respect. What is present and living in their environment is their proper material. The influences that have formed the writer are identical with those which have moulded the events that constitute the matter of his story. The author's spirit, and that of the actions he narrates, is one and the same. He describes scenes in which he himself has been an actor, or at any rate an interested spectator. It is short periods of time, individual shapes of persons and occurrences, single, unreflected traits, of which he makes his picture. And his aim is nothing more than the presentation to posterity of an image of events as clear as that which he himself possessed in virtue of personal observation, or life-like descriptions. Reflections are none of his business, for he lives in the spirit of his subject; he has not attained an elevation above it. If, as in Caesar's case, he belongs to the exalted rank of generals or statesmen, it is the prosecution of *his own aims* that constitutes the history.

Such speeches as we find in Thucydides (for example) of which we can positively assert that they are not *bona fide* reports, would seem to make against out statement that a historian of his class presents us no reflected picture; that persons and people appear in his works in *propria persona*. Speeches, it must be allowed, are veritable transactions in the human commonwealth; in fact, very gravely influential transactions. It is indeed, often said, "Such and such things are only talk;" by way of demonstrating their harmlessness. That for which this excuse is brought may be mere "talk"; and talk enjoys the important privilege of being harmless. But addresses of peoples to peoples, or orations directed to nations and to princes, are integrant constituents of history. Granted that such orations as those of Pericles – that most profoundly accomplished, genuine, noble statesman – were elaborated by Thucydides, it must yet be maintained that they were not foreign to the character of the speaker. In the orations in question, these men proclaim the maxims adopted by their countrymen, and which formed their own character; they record their views of their political relations, and of their moral and spiritual nature; and the principles of their designs and conduct. What the historian puts into their mouths is no supposititious system of ideas, but an uncorrupted transcript of their intellectual and moral habitudes.

Of these historians, whom we must make thoroughly our own, with whom we must linger long, if we would live with their respective nations, and enter deeply into their spirit: of these historians, to whose pages we may turn not for the purposes of erudition merely, but with a view to deep and genuine enjoyment, there are fewer than might be imagined. Herodotus the *Father,* i.e., the *Founder* of History, and Thucydides have been already mentioned. Xenophon's *Retreat of the Ten Thousand,* is a work equally original. Caesar's *Commentaries* are the simple masterpiece of a mighty spirit. Among the ancients, these annalists were necessarily great captains and statesmen. In the Middle Ages, if we except the Bishops, who were placed in the very centre of the political world, the Monks monopolize this category as naive chroniclers who were as decidedly *isolated* from active life as those elder annalists had been connected with it. In modern times the relations are entirely altered. Our culture is essentially comprehensive, and immediately changes all events into historical representations. Belonging to the class in question, we have vivid, simple, clear narrations – especially of military transactions – which might fairly take their place with those of Caesar. In richness of matter and fulness of detail as regards strategic appliances, and attendant circumstances, they are even more instructive. The French "Mémoires," also, fall under this category. In many cases these are written by men of mark, though relating to affairs of little note. They not unfrequently contain a large proportion of anecdotal matter, so that the ground they occupy is narrow and trivial. Yet they are often veritable masterpieces in history; as those of Cardinal de Retz, which in fact trench on a larger historical field. In Germany such masters are rare.

Frederick the Great ("Histoire de Mon Temps") is an illustrious exception. Writers of this order must occupy an elevated position. Only from such a position is it possible to take an extensive view of affairs – to see everything. This is out of the question for him, who from below merely gets a glimpse of the great world through a miserable cranny.

II. The second kind of history we may call the *reflective*. It is history whose mode of representation is not really confined by the limits of the time to which it relates, but whose spirit transcends the present. In this second order a strongly marked variety of species may be distinguished.

1. It is the aim of the investigator to gain a view of the entire history of a people or a country, or of the world, in short, what we call *Universal History*. In this case the working up of the historical material is the main point. The workman approaches his task with *his own* spirit; a spirit distinct from that of the element he is to manipulate. Here a very important consideration will be the principles to which the author refers the bearing and motives of the actions and events which he describes, and those which determine the form of his narrative. Among us Germans this reflective treatment and the display of ingenuity which it occasions assume a manifold variety of phases. Every writer of history proposes to himself an original method. The English and French confess to general principles of historical composition. Their standpoint is more that of cosmopolitan or of national culture. Among us each labors to invent a purely individual point of view. Instead of writing history, we are always beating our brains to discover how history ought to be written. This first kind of Reflective History is most nearly akin to the preceding, when it has no farther aim than to present the annals of a country complete. Such compilations (among which may be reckoned the works of Livy, Diodorus Siculus, Johannes von Müller's History of Switzerland) are, if well performed, highly meritorious.

Among the best of the kind may be reckoned such annalists as approach those of the first class; who give so vivid a transcript of events that the reader may well fancy himself listening to contemporaries and eye-witnesses. But it often happens that the individuality of tone which must characterize a writer belonging to a different culture is not modified in accordance with the periods such a record must traverse. The spirit of the writer is quite other than that of the times of which he treats. Thus Livy puts into the mouths of the old Roman kings, consuls, and generals such orations as would be delivered by an accomplished advocate of the Livian era, and which strikingly contrast with the genuine traditions of Roman antiquity (*e.g.,* the fable of Menenius Agrippa). In the same way he gives us descriptions of battles, as if he had been an actual spectator; but whose features would serve well enough for battles in any period, and whose distinctness contrasts on the other hand with the want of connection and the inconsistency that prevail elsewhere, even in his treatment of chief points of interest. The difference between such a compiler and an original historian may be best seen by comparing Polybius himself with the style in which Livy uses, expands, and abridges his annals in those periods of which Polybius's account has been preserved. Johannes von Müller has given a stiff, formal, pedantic aspect to his history, in the endeavor to remain faithful in his portraiture to the times he describes. We much prefer the narratives we find in old Tschudy. All is more naive and natural than it appears in the garb of a fictitious and affected archaism.

A history which aspires to traverse long periods of time, or to be universal, must indeed forego the attempt to give individual representations of the past as it actually existed. It must foreshorten its pictures by abstractions; and this includes not merely the omission of events and deeds, but whatever is involved in the fact that Thought is, after all, the most trenchant epitomist. A battle, a great victory, a siege, no longer maintains its original proportions, but is put off with a bare mention. When Livy, *e.g.,* tells us of the wars with the Volsci, we sometimes have the brief announcement: "This year war was carried on with the Volsci."

2. A second species of Reflective History is what we may call the *Pragmatical.* When we have to deal with the Past, and occupy ourselves with a remote world, a Present rises into being for the mind – produced by its own activity, as the reward of its labor. The occurrences are, indeed, various; but the idea which pervades them – their deeper import and connection – is *one.* This takes the occurrence out of the category of the Past and makes it virtually Present. Pragmatical (didactic) reflections, though in their nature decidedly abstract, are truly and indefeasibly of

19

the Present, and quicken the annals of the dead Past with the life of to-day. Whether, indeed, such reflections are truly interesting and enlivening, depends on the writer's own spirit. Moral reflections must here be specially noticed – the moral teaching expected from history; which latter has not infrequently been treated with a direct view to the former. It may be allowed that examples of virtue elevate the soul, and are applicable in the moral instruction of children for impressing excellence upon their minds. But the destinies of peoples and states, their interests, relations, and the complicated tissue of their affairs, present quite another field. Rulers, Statesmen, Nations, are wont to be emphatically commended to the teaching which experience offers in history. But what experience and history teach is this – that peoples and governments never have learned anything from history, or acted on principles deduced from it. Each period is involved in such peculiar circumstances, exhibits a condition of things so strictly idiosyncratic, that its conduct must be regulated by considerations connected with itself, and itself alone. Amid the pressure of great events, a general principle gives no help. It is useless to revert to similar circumstances in the Past. The pallid shades of memory struggle in vain with the life and freedom of the Present. Looked at in this light, nothing can be shallower than the oft-repeated appeal to Greek and Roman examples during the French Revolution. Nothing is more diverse than the genius of those nations and that of our times. Johannes v. Müller, in his "Universal History," as also in his "History of Switzerland," had such moral aims in view. He designed to prepare a body of political doctrines for the instruction of princes, governments, and peoples (he formed a special collection of doctrines and reflections – frequently giving us in his correspondence the exact number of apophthegms which he had compiled in a week); but he cannot reckon this part of his labor as among the best that he accomplished. It is only a thorough, liberal, comprehensive view of historical relations (such e.g., as we find in Montesquieu's "Esprit des Lois") that can give truth and interest to reflections of this order. One Reflective History, therefore, supersedes another. The materials are patent to every writer: each is likely enough to believe himself capable of arranging and manipulating them; and we may expect that each will insist upon his own spirit as that of the age in question. Disgusted by such reflective histories, readers have often

20

returned with pleasure to a narrative adopting no particular point of view. These certainly have their value; but for the most part they offer only material for history. We Germans are content with such. The French, on the other hand, display great genius in reanimating bygone times, and in bringing the past to bear upon the present condition of things. [3] The third form of Reflective History is the *Critical.* This deserves mention as pre-eminently the mode of treating history now current in Germany. It is not history itself that is here presented. We might more properly designate it as a History of History; a criticism of historical narratives and an investigation of their truth and credibility. Its peculiarity in point of fact and of intention, consists in the acuteness with which the writer extorts something from the records which was not in the matters recorded. The French have given us much that is profound and judicious in this class of composition. But they have not endeavored to pass a merely critical procedure for substantial history. They have duly presented their judgments in the form of critical treatises. Among us, the so-called "higher criticism," which reigns supreme in the domain of philology, has also taken possession of our historical literature. This "higher criticism" has been the pretext for introducing all the anti-historical monstrosities that a vain imagination could suggest. Here we have the other method of making the past a living reality; putting subjective fancies in the place of historical data; fancies whose merit is measured by their boldness, that is, the scantiness of the particulars on which they are based, and the peremptoriness with which they contravene the best established facts of history.[4] The last species of Reflective History announces its fragmentary character on the very face of it. It adopts an abstract position; yet, since it takes general points of view (*e.g.,* as the History of Art, of Law, of Religion), it forms a transition to the Philosophical History of the World. In our time this form of the history of ideas has been more developed and brought into notice. Such branches of national life stand in close relation to the entire complex of a people's annals; and the question of chief importance in relation to our subject is, whether the connection of the whole is exhibited in its truth and reality, or referred to merely external relations. In the latter case, these important phenomena (Art, Law, Religion, etc.) appear *as* purely accidental national peculiarities. It must be remarked that, when Reflective History has advanced to the adoption of general points of view, if the position taken is a true one, these are found to constitute – not a merely external thread, a superficial series – but are the inward guiding soul of the occurrences and actions that occupy a nation's annals. For, like the soul-conductor Mercury, the Idea is in truth, the leader of peoples and of the World; and Spirit, the rational and necessitated will of that conductor, is and has been the director of the events of the World's History. To become acquainted with Spirit in this its office of guidance, is the object of our present undertaking. This brings us to

III. The third kind of history – the *Philosophical.* No explanation was needed of the two previous classes; their nature was self-evident. It is otherwise with this last, which certainly seems to require an exposition or justification. The most general definition that can be given, is, that the Philosophy of History means nothing but the *thoughtful consideration of it.* Thought is, indeed, essential to humanity. It is this that distinguishes us from the brutes. In sensation, cognition, and intellection; in our instincts and volitions, as far as they are truly human, Thought is an invariable element. To insist upon Thought in this connection with history may, however, appear unsatisfactory. In this science it would seem as if Thought must be subordinate to what is given, to the realities of fact; that this is its basis and guide: while Philosophy dwells in the region of self-produced ideas, without reference to actuality. Approaching history thus prepossessed, Speculation might be expected to treat it as a mere passive material; and, so far from leaving it in its native truth, to force it into conformity with a tyrannous idea, and to construe it, as the phrase is, "à *priori.*" But as it is the business of history simply to adopt into its records what is and has been – actual occurrences and transactions; and since it remains true to its character in proportion as it strictly adheres to its data, we seem to have in Philosophy, a process diametrically opposed to that of the historiographer. This contradiction, and the charge consequently brought against speculation, shall be explained and confuted. We do not, however, propose to correct the innumerable special misrepresentations, trite or novel, that are current respecting the aims, the interests, and the modes of treating history, and its relation to Philosophy.

The only Thought which Philosophy brings with it to the contemplation of History, is the simple conception of *Reason;* that Reason is the

22

Sovereign of the World; that the history of the world, therefore, presents us with a rational process. This conviction and intuition is a hypothesis in the domain of history as such. In that of Philosophy it is no hypothesis. It is there proved by speculative cognition, that Reason – and this term may here suffice us, without investigating the relation sustained by the Universe to the Divine Being – is *Substance,* as well as *Infinite Power;* its own *Infinite Material* underlying all the natural and spiritual life which it originates, as also the *Infinite Form* – that which sets this Material in motion. On the one hand, Reason is the *substance* of the Universe; viz., that by which and in which all reality has its being and subsistence. On the other hand, it is the *Infinite Energy* of the Universe; since Reason is not so powerless as to be incapable of producing anything but a mere ideal, a mere intention – having its place outside reality, nobody knows where; something separate and abstract, in the heads of certain human beings. It is *the infinite complex of things,* their entire Essence and Truth. It is its own material which it commits to its own Active Energy to work up; not needing, as finite action does, the conditions of an external material of given means from which it may obtain its support, and the objects of its activity. It supplies its own nourishment, and is the object of its own operations. While it is exclusively its own basis of existence, and absolute final aim, it is also the energizing power realizing this aim; developing it not only in the phenomena of the Natural, but also of the Spiritual Universe – the History of the World. That this "Idea" or "Reason" is the *True,* the *Eternal,* the absolutely *powerful* essence; that it reveals itself in the World, and that in that World nothing else is revealed but this and its honor and glory – is the thesis which, as we have said, has been proved in Philosophy, and is here regarded as demonstrated.

In those of my hearers who are not acquainted with Philosophy, I may fairly presume, at least, the existence of a *belief* in Reason, a desire, a thirst for acquaintance with it, in entering upon this course of Lectures. It is, in fact, the wish for rational insight, not the ambition to amass a mere heap of acquirements, that should be presupposed in every case as possessing the mind of the learner in the study of science. If the clear idea of Reason is not already developed in our minds, in beginning the study of Universal History, we should at least have the firm, unconquerable faith that Reason *does* exist there; and that the World of intelligence and conscious volition is not abandoned to chance, but must show itself in the light of the self-cognizant Idea. Yet *I* am not obliged to make any such preliminary demand upon your faith. What I have said thus provisionally, and what I shall have further to say, is, even in reference to *our* branch of science, not to be regarded as hypothetical, but as a summary view of the whole; the *result of the investigation* we are about to pursue; a result which happens to be known to *me,* because I have traversed the entire field. It is only an inference from the history of the World, that its development has been a rational process; that the history in question has constituted the rational necessary course of the World-Spirit – that Spirit whose nature is always one and the same, but which unfolds this its one nature in the phenomena of the World's existence. This must, as before stated, present itself as the ultimate *result* of History. But we have to take the latter as it is. We must proceed historically – empirically. Among other precautions we must take care not to be misled by professed historians who (especially among the Germans, and enjoying a considerable authority), are chargeable with the very procedure of which they accuse the Philosopher – introducing *à priori* inventions of their own into the records of the Past. It is, for example, a widely current fiction, that there was an original primeval people, taught immediately by God, endowed with perfect insight and wisdom, possessing a thorough knowledge of all natural laws and spiritual truth; that there have been such or such sacerdotal peoples; or, to mention a more specific averment, that there was a Roman Epos, from which the Roman historians derived the early annals of their city, etc. Authorities of this kind we leave to those talented historians by profession, among whom (in Germany at least) their use is not uncommon. – We might then announce it as the first condition to be observed, that we should faithfully adopt all that is historical. But in such general expressions themselves, as "faithfully" and "adopt," lies the ambiguity. Even the ordinary, the "impartial" historiographer, who believes and professes that he maintains a simply receptive attitude; surrendering himself only to the data supplied him – is by no means passive as regards the exercise of his thinking powers. He brings his categories with him, and sees the phenomena presented to his mental vision, exclusively through these media. And, especially in all that

24

pretends to the name of science, it is indispensable that Reason should not sleep – that reflection should be in full play. To him who looks upon the world rationally, the world in its turn presents a rational aspect. The relation is mutual. But the various exercises of reflection – the different points of view – the modes of deciding the simple question of the relative importance of events (the first category that occupies the attention of the historian), do not belong to this place.

I will only mention two phases and points of view that concern the generally diffused conviction that Reason has ruled, and is still ruling in the world, and consequently in the world's history; because they give us, at the same time, an opportunity for more closely investigating the question that presents the greatest difficulty, and for indicating a branch of the subject, which will have to be enlarged on in the sequel. I. One of these points is, that passage in history, which informs us that the Greek Anaxagoras was the first to enunciate the doctrine that νουσ, Understanding generally, or Reason, governs the world. It is not intelligence as self-conscious Reason – not a Spirit as such that is meant; and we must clearly distinguish these from each other. The movement of the solar system takes place according to unchangeable laws. These laws are Reason, implicit in the phenomena in question. But neither the sun nor the planets, which revolve around it according to these laws, can be said to have any consciousness of them.

A thought of this kind – that Nature is an embodiment of Reason; that it is unchangeably subordinate to universal laws, appears nowise striking or strange to us. We are accustomed to such conceptions, and find nothing extraordinary in them. And I have mentioned this extraordinary occurrence, partly to show how history teaches, that ideas of this kind, which may seem trivial to us, have not always been in the world; that, on the contrary, such a thought makes an epoch in the annals of human intelligence. Aristotle says of Anaxagoras, as the originator of the thought in question, that he appeared as a sober man among the drunken. Socrates adopted the doctrine from Anaxagoras, and it forthwith became the ruling idea in Philosophy – except in the school of Epicurus, who ascribed all events to chance. "I was delighted with the sentiment" – Plato makes Socrates say – "and hoped I had found a teacher who would show me Nature in harmony with Reason, who would demonstrate in

25

each particular phenomenon its specific aim, and in the whole, the grand object of the Universe. I would not have surrendered this hope for a great deal. But how very much was I disappointed, when, having zealously applied myself to the writings of Anaxagoras, I found that he adduces only external causes, such as Atmosphere, Ether, Water, and the like." It is evident that the defect which Socrates complains of respecting Anaxagoras's doctrine, does not concern the principle itself, but the shortcoming of the propounder in applying it to Nature in the concrete. Nature is not deduced from that principle: the latter remains in fact a mere abstraction, inasmuch as the former is not comprehended and exhibited as a development of it – an organization produced by and from Reason. I wish, at the very outset, to call your attention to the important difference between a conception, a principle, a truth limited to an *abstract* form and its determinate application, and concrete development. This distinction affects the whole fabric of philosophy; and among other bearings of it there is one to which we shall have to revert at the close of our view of Universal History, in investigating the aspect of political affairs in the most recent period.

We have next to notice the rise of this idea – that Reason directs the World – in connection with a further application of it, well known to us – in the form, viz., of the *religious truth,* that the world is not abandoned to chance and external contingent causes, but that a *Providence* controls it. I stated above, that I would not make a demand on your faith, in regard to the principle announced. Yet I might appeal to your belief in it, *in this religious aspect,* if, as a general rule, the nature of philosophical science allowed it to attach authority to presuppositions. To put it in another shape – this appeal is forbidden, because the science of which we have to treat, proposes itself to furnish the proof (not indeed of the abstract *Truth* of the doctrine, but) of its correctness as compared with facts. The truth, then, that a Providence (that of God) presides over the events of the World – consorts with the proposition in question; for *Divine* Providence is Wisdom, endowed with an infinite Power, which realizes its aim, viz., the absolute rational design of the World. Reason is Thought conditioning itself with perfect freedom. But a difference – rather a contradiction – will manifest itself, between this belief and our principle, just as was the case in reference to the demand made by

26

Socrates in the case of Anaxagoras's dictum. For that belief is similarly indefinite; it is what is called a belief in a general Providence, and is not followed out into definite application, or displayed in its bearing on the grand total – the entire course of human history. But to *explain* History is to depict the passions of mankind, the genius, the active powers, that play their part on the great stage; and the providentially determined process which these exhibit, constitutes what is generally called the "plan" of Providence. Yet it is this very plan which is supposed to be concealed from our view: which it is deemed presumption, even to wish to recognize. The ignorance of Anaxagoras, as to how intelligence reveals itself in actual existence, was ingenuous. Neither in his consciousness, nor in that of Greece at large, had that thought been farther expanded. He had not attained the power to apply his general principle to the concrete, so as to deduce the latter from the former. It was Socrates who took the first step in comprehending the union of the Concrete with the Universal. Anaxagoras, then, did not take up a *hostile* position toward such an application. The common belief in Providence *does;* at least it opposes the use of the principle on the large scale, and denies the possibility of discerning the plan of Providence. In isolated cases this plan is supposed to be manifest. Pious persons are encouraged to recognize in particular circumstances, something more than mere chance; to acknowledge the guiding hand of God; *e.g.,* when help has unexpectedly come to an individual in great perplexity and need. But these instances of providential design are of a limited kind, and concern the accomplishment of nothing more than the desires of the individual in question. But in the history of the World, the *Individuals* we have to do with are *Peoples;* Totalities that are States. We cannot, therefore, be satisfied with what we may call this "peddling" view of Providence, to which the belief alluded to limits itself. Equally unsatisfactory is the merely abstract, undefined belief in a Providence, when that belief is not brought to bear upon the details of the process which it conducts. On the contrary our earnest endeavor must be directed to the recognition of the ways of Providence, the means it uses, and the historical phenomena in which it manifests itself; and we must show their connection with the general principle above mentioned. But in noticing the recognition of the plan of Divine Providence generally, I have implicitly touched upon a prominent question of the day; viz., that of the possibility of knowing

God: or rather – since public opinion has ceased to allow it to be a matter of *question* – the *doctrine* that it is impossible to know God. In direct contravention of what is commanded in holy Scripture as the highest duty – that we should not merely love, but *know* God – the prevalent dogma involves the denial of what is there said; viz., that it is the Spirit (der Geist) that leads into Truth, knows all things, penetrates even into the deep things of the Godhead. While the Divine Being is thus placed beyond our knowledge, and outside the limit of all human things, we have the convenient license of wandering as far as we list, in the direction of our own fancies. We are freed from the obligation to refer our knowledge to the Divine and True. On the other hand, the vanity and egotism which characterize it find, in this false position, ample justification; and the pious modesty which puts far from it the knowledge of God can well estimate how much furtherance thereby accrues to its own wayward and vain strivings. I have been unwilling to leave out of sight the connection between our thesis – that Reason governs and has governed the World – and the question of the possibility of a knowledge of God, chiefly that I might not lose the opportunity of mentioning the imputation against Philosophy of being shy of noticing religious truths, or of having occasion to be so; in which is insinuated the suspicion that it has anything but a clear conscience in the presence of these truths. So far from this being the case, the fact is, that in recent times Philosophy has been obliged to defend the domain of religion against the attacks of several theological systems. In the Christian religion God has revealed Himself – that is, he has given us to understand what He is; so that He is no longer a concealed or secret existence. And this possibility of knowing Him, thus afforded us, renders such knowledge a duty. God wishes no narrow-hearted souls or empty heads for his children; but those whose spirit is of itself indeed poor, but rich in the knowledge of Him; and who regard this knowledge of God as the only valuable possession. That development of the thinking spirit which has resulted from the revelation of the Divine Being as its original basis must ultimately advance to the *intellectual* comprehension of what was presented in the first instance, to *feeling* and *imagination*. The time must eventually come for understanding that rich product of active Reason, which the History of the World offers to us. It was for awhile the fashion to profess admiration for the wisdom of God as displayed in animals, plants, and isolated occurrences. But, if it be allowed that Providence manifests itself in such objects and forms of existence, why not also in Universal History? This is deemed too great a matter to be thus regarded. But Divine Wisdom, *i.e.,* Reason, is one and the same in the great as in the little; and we must not imagine God to be too weak to exercise his wisdom on the grand scale. Our intellectual striving aims at realizing the conviction that what was *intended* by eternal wisdom, is actually *accomplished* in the domain of existent, active Spirit, as well as in that of mere Nature. Our mode of treating the subject is, in this aspect, a Theodicaea – a justification of the ways of God – which Leibnitz attempted metaphysically, in his method, *i.e.,* in indefinite abstract categories – so that the ill that is found in the World may be comprehended, and the thinking Spirit reconciled with the fact of the existence of evil. Indeed, nowhere is such a harmonizing view more pressingly demanded than in Universal History; and it can be attained only by recognizing the *positive* existence, in which that negative element is a subordinate, and vanquished nullity. On the one hand, the ultimate design of the World must be perceived; and, on the other hand, the fact that this design has been actually realized in it, and that evil has not been able permanently to assert a competing position. But this superintending vows, or in "Providence." "Reason," whose sovereignty over the World has been maintained, is as indefinite a term as "Providence," supposing the term to be used by those who are unable to characterize it distinctly – to show wherein it consists, so as to enable us to decide whether a thing is rational or irrational. An adequate definition of Reason is the first desideratum; and whatever boast may be made of strict adherence to it in explaining phenomena – without such a definition we get no farther than mere words. With these observations we may proceed to the second point of view that has to be considered in this Introduction.

II. The inquiry into the *essential destiny* of Reason – as far as it is considered in reference to the World – is identical with the question, *what is the ultimate design of the World?* And the expression implies that that design is destined to be realized. Two points of consideration suggest themselves; first, the *import* of this design – its abstract definition; and secondly, its *realization.*

29

It must be observed at the outset, that the phenomenon we investigate – Universal History – belongs to the realm of *Spirit.* The term " *World,*" includes both physical and psychical Nature. Physical Nature also plays its part in the World's History, and attention will have to be paid to the fundamental natural relations thus involved. But Spirit, and the course of its development, is our substantial object. Our task does not require us to contemplate Nature as a Rational System in itself – though in its own proper domain it proves itself such – but simply in its relation to *Spirit.* On the stage on which we are observing it – Universal History – Spirit displays itself in its most concrete reality. Notwithstanding this (or rather for the very purpose of comprehending the *general* principles which this, its form of *concrete reality,* embodies) we must premise some abstract characteristics of the *nature of Spirit.* Such an explanation, however, cannot be given here under any other form than that of bare assertion. The present is not the occasion for unfolding the idea of Spirit speculatively; for whatever has a place in an Introduction, must, as already observed, be taken as simply historical; something assumed as having been explained and proved elsewhere; or whose demonstration awaits the sequel of the Science of History itself. We have therefore to mention here: (1) The abstract characteristics of the nature of Spirit. (2) What means Spirit uses in order to realize its Idea. (3) Lastly, we must consider the shape which the perfect embodiment of Spirit assumes – the State, (1) The nature of Spirit may be understood *by* a glance at its direct opposite – *Matter. As* the essence of Matter is Gravity, so, on the other hand, we may affirm that the substance, the essence of Spirit is Freedom. All will readily assent to the doctrine that Spirit, among other properties, is also endowed with Freedom; but philosophy teaches that all the qualities of Spirit exist only through Freedom; that all are but means for attaining Freedom; that all seek and produce this and this alone. It is a result of speculative Philosophy that Freedom is the sole truth of Spirit. Matter possesses gravity in virtue of its tendency toward a central point. It is essentially composite; consisting of parts that *exclude* each other. It seeks its Unity; and therefore exhibits itself as self-destructive, as verging toward its opposite [an indivisible point]. If it could attain this, it would be Matter no longer, it would have perished. It strives after the realization of its Idea; for in Unity it exists *ideally.* Spirit, on the contrary, may be defined as that which has its centre in itself. It has not a unity

30

outside itself, but has already found it; it exists *in* and *with itself.* Matter has its essence out of itself; Spirit is *self-contained existence* (*Bei-sich-selbst-seyn*). Now this is Freedom, exactly. For if I am dependent, my being is referred to something else which I am not; I cannot exist independently of something external. I am free, on the contrary, when my existence depends upon myself. This self-contained existence of Spirit is none other than self-consciousness – consciousness of one's own being. Two things must be distinguished in consciousness; first, the fact *that I know;* secondly, *what I know.* In *self* consciousness these are merged in one; for Spirit *knows itself.* It involves an appreciation of its own nature, as also an energy enabling it to realize itself; to make itself *actually* that which it is *potentially.* According to this abstract definition it may be said of Universal History, that it is the exhibition of Spirit in the process of working out the knowledge of that which it is potentially. And as the germ bears in itself the whole nature of the tree, and the taste and form of its fruits, so do the first traces of Spirit virtually contain the whole of that History. The Orientals have not attained the knowledge that Spirit – Man *as such* – is free; and because they do not know this, they are not free. They only know that *one is free.* But on this very account, the freedom of that one is only caprice; ferocity – brutal recklessness of passion, or a mildness and tameness of the desires, which is itself only an accident of Nature – mere caprice like the former. – That *one* is therefore only a Despot; not a *free man.* The consciousness of Freedom first arose among the Greeks, and therefore they were free; but they, and the Romans likewise, knew only that *some* are free – not man as such. Even Plato and Aristotle did not know this. The Greeks, therefore, had slaves; and their whole life and the maintenance of their splendid liberty, was implicated with the institution of slavery: a fact moreover, which made that liberty on the one hand only an accidental, transient and limited growth; on the other hand, constituted it a rigorous thraldom of our common nature – of the Human. The German nations, under the influence of Christianity, were the first to attain the consciousness that man, as man, is free: that it is the *freedom* of Spirit which constitutes its essence. This consciousness arose first in religion, the inmost region of Spirit; but to introduce the principle into the various relations of the actual world involves a more extensive problem than its simple implantation; a problem whose solution and application require a severe and lengthened process of culture. In proof of this, we may note that slavery did not cease immediately on the reception of Christianity. Still less did liberty predominate in States; or Governments and Constitutions adopt a rational organization, or recognize freedom as their basis. That application of the principle to political relations; the thorough moulding and interpenetration of the constitution of society by it, is a process identical with history itself. I have already directed attention to the distinction here involved, between a principle as such, and its *application; i.e.,* its introduction and carrying out in the actual phenomena of Spirit and Life. This is a point of fundamental importance in our science, and one which must be constantly respected as essential. And in the same way as this distinction has attracted attention in view of the *Christian* principle of selfconsciousness – Freedom; it also shows itself as an essential one, in view of the principle of Freedom *generally.* The History of the world is none other than the progress of the consciousness of Freedom; a progress whose development according to the necessity of its nature, it is our business to investigate. The general statement given above, of the various grades in the consciousness of Freedom – and which we applied in the first instance to the fact that the Eastern nations knew only that *one* is free; the Greek and Roman world only that *some* are free; while *we* know that all men absolutely (man *as man)* are free – supplies us with the natural division of Universal History, and suggests the mode of its discussion. This is remarked, however, only incidentally and anticipatively; some other ideas must be first explained.

The destiny of the spiritual World, and – since this is the *substantial World,* while the physical remains subordinate to it, or, in the language of speculation, has no truth *as against* the spiritual – *the final cause of the World at large,* we allege to be the *consciousness* of its own freedom on the part of Spirit, and *ipso facto,* the *reality* of that freedom. But that this term "Freedom," without further qualification, is an indefinite, and incalculable ambiguous term; and that while that which it represents is the *ne plus ultra* of attainment, it is liable to an infinity of misunderstandings, confusions and errors, and to become the occasion for all imaginable excesses – has never been more clearly known and felt than in modern times. Yet, for the present, we must content ourselves with the term itself without farther definition. Attention was also directed to the importance of the infinite difference between a principle in the abstract, and its realization in the concrete. In the process before us, the essential nature of freedom – which involves in it absolute necessity – is to be displayed as coming to a consciousness of itself (for it is in its very nature, self-consciousness) and thereby realizing its existence. Itself is its own object of attainment, and the sole aim of Spirit. This result it is, at which the process of the World's History has been continually aiming; and to which the sacrifices that have ever and anon been laid on the vast altar of the earth, through the long lapse of ages, have been offered. This is the only aim that sees itself realized and fulfilled; the only pole of repose amid the ceaseless change of events and conditions, and the sole efficient principle that pervades them. This final aim is God's purpose with the world; but God is the absolutely perfect Being, and can, therefore, will nothing other than himself – his own Will. The Nature of His Will – that is, His Nature itself – is what we here call the Idea of Freedom; translating the language of Religion into that of Thought. The question, then, which we may next put is: What means does this principle of Freedom use for its realization? This is the second point we have to consider. (2) The question of the *means* by which Freedom develops itself to a World, conducts us to the phenomenon of History itself. Although Freedom is, primarily, an undeveloped idea, the means it uses are external and phenomenal; presenting themselves in History to our sensuous vision. The first glance at History convinces us that the actions of men proceed from their needs, their passions, their characters and talents; and impresses us with the belief that such needs, passions and interests are the sole springs of action – the efficient agents in this scene of activity. Among these may, perhaps, be found aims of a liberal or universal kind – benevolence it may be, or noble patriotism; but such virtues and general views are but insignificant as compared with the World and its doings. We may perhaps see the Ideal of Reason actualized in those who adopt such aims, and within the sphere of their influence; but they bear only a trifling proportion to the mass of the human race; and the extent of that influence is limited accordingly. Passions, private aims, and the satisfaction of selfish desires, are on the other hand, most effective springs of action. Their power lies in the fact that they respect none of the limitations which justice and morality would impose on them; and that these natural impulses have a more direct influence over man than the artificial and tedious discipline that tends to order and self-restraint, law and morality. When we look at this display of passions, and the consequences of their violence; the Unreason which is associated not only with them, but even (rather we might say *especially*) with *good* designs and righteous aims; when we see the evil, the vice, the ruin that has befallen the most flourishing kingdoms which the mind of man ever created; we can scarce avoid being filled with sorrow at this universal taint of corruption: and, since this decay is not the work of mere Nature, but of the Human Will – a moral embitterment – a revolt of the Good Spirit (if it have a place within us) may well be the result of our reflections. Without rhetorical exaggeration, a simply truthful combination of the miseries that have overwhelmed the noblest of nations and polities, and the finest exemplars of private virtue – forms a picture of most fearful aspect, and excites emotions of the profoundest and most hopeless sadness, counterbalanced by no consolatory result. We endure in beholding it a mental torture, allowing no defence or escape but the consideration that what has happened could not be otherwise; that it is a fatality which no intervention could alter. And at last we draw back from the intolerable disgust with which these sorrowful reflections threaten us, into the more agreeable environment of our individual life – the Present formed by our private aims and interests. In short we retreat into the selfishness that stands on the quiet shore, and thence enjoys in safety the distant spectacle of "wrecks confusedly hurled." But even regarding History as the slaughter-bench at which the happiness of peoples, the wisdom of States, and the virtue of individuals have been victimized – the question involuntarily arises – to what principle, to what final aim these enormous sacrifices have been offered. From this point the investigation usually proceeds to that which we have made the general commencement of our inquiry. Starting from this we pointed out those phenomena which made up a picture so suggestive of gloomy emotions and thoughtful reflections – as *the very field* which we, for our part, regard as exhibiting only the means for realizing what we assert to be the essential destiny – the absolute aim, or – which comes to the same thing – the true *result* of the World's History. We have all along purposely eschewed "moral reflections" as a method of rising from the scene of historical specialties to the general principles

34

which they embody. Besides, it is not the interest of such sentimentalities, really to rise above those depressing emotions; and to solve the enigmas of Providence which the considerations that occasioned them, present. It is essential to their character to find a gloomy satisfaction in the empty and fruitless sublimities of that negative result. We return them to the point of view which we have adopted; observing that the successive steps (*momente*) of the analysis to which it will lead us, will also evolve the conditions requisite for answering the inquiries suggested by the panorama of sin and suffering that history unfolds.

The *first* remark we have to make, and which – though already presented more than once – cannot be too often repeated when the occasion seems to call for it – is that what we call *principle, aim, destiny,* or the nature and idea of Spirit, is something merely general and abstract. Principle – Plan of Existence – Law – is a hidden, undeveloped essence, which *as such* – however true in itself – is not completely real. Aims, principles, etc., have a place in our thoughts, in our subjective design only; but not yet in the sphere of reality. That which exists for itself only, is a possibility, a potentiality; but has not yet emerged into Existence. A *second* element must be introduced in order to produce actuality – viz., actuation, realization; and whose motive power *is* the Will – the activity of man in the widest sense. It is only by this activity that that Idea as well as abstract characteristics generally, are realized, actualized; for of themselves they are powerless. The motive power that puts them in operation, and gives them determinate existence, is the need, instinct, inclination, and passion of man. That some conception of mine should be developed into act and existence, is my earnest desire: I wish to assert my personality in connection with it: I wish to be satisfied by its execution. If I am to exert myself for any object, it must in some way or other be *my* object. In the accomplishment of such or such designs I must at the same time find *my* satisfaction; although the purpose for which I exert myself includes a complication of results, many of which have no interest for me. This is the absolute right of personal existence – to find *itself* satisfied in its activity and labor. If men are to interest themselves for anything, they must (so to speak) have part of their existence involved in it; find their individuality gratified by its attainment. Here a mistake must be avoided. We intend blame, and justly impute it as a fault, when we say of an individual, that he is "interested" (in taking part in such or such transactions), that is, seeks only his private advantage. In reprehending this we find fault with him for furthering his personal aims without any regard to a more comprehensive design; of which he takes advantage to promote his own interest, or which he even sacrifices with this view. But he who is active in *promoting an object* is not simply "interested," but interested in that object itself. Language faithfully expresses this distinction. – Nothing therefore happens, nothing is accomplished, unless the individuals concerned, seek their own satisfaction in the issue. They are particular units of society; *i.e.,* they have special needs, instincts, and interests generally, peculiar to themselves. Among these needs are not only such as we usually call necessities – the stimuli of individual desire and volition – but also those connected with individual views and convictions; or – to use a term expressing less decision – leanings of opinion; supposing the impulses of reflection, understanding, and reason, to have been awakened. In these cases people demand, if they are to exert themselves in any direction, that the object should commend itself to them; that in point of opinion – whether as to its goodness, justice, advantage, profit – they should be able to "enter into it" (*dabei seyn*). This is a consideration of especial importance in our age, when people are less than formerly influenced by reliance on others, and by authority; when, on the contrary, they devote their activities to a cause on the ground of their own understanding, their independent conviction and opinion.

We assert then that nothing has been accomplished without interest on the part of the actors; and – if interest be called passion, inasmuch as the whole individuality, to the neglect of all other actual or possible interests and claims, is devoted to an object with every fibre of volition, concentrating all its desires and powers upon it – we may affirm absolutely that *nothing great in the World* has been accomplished without *passion.* Two elements, therefore, enter into the object of our investigation; the first the Idea, the second the complex of human passions; the one the warp, the other the woof of the vast arras-web of Universal History. The concrete mean and union of the two is Liberty, under the conditions of morality in a State. We have spoken of the Idea of Freedom as the nature of Spirit, and the absolute goal of History. Passion is regarded as a thing of sinister aspect, as more or less immoral. Man is required to have no passions. Passion, it is true, is not quite the suitable word for what I wish to express. I mean here nothing more than the human activity as resulting from private interests – special, or if you will, selfseeking designs – with this qualification, that the whole energy of will and character is devoted to their attainment; that other interests (which would in themselves constitute attractive aims) or rather all things else, are sacrificed to them. The object in question is so bound up with the man's will, that it entirely and alone determines the "hue of resolution," and is inseparable from it. It has become the very essence of his volition. For a person is a specific existence; not man in general (a term to which no real existence corresponds) but a particular human being. The term "character" likewise expresses this idiosyncrasy of Will and Intelligence. But *Character* comprehends all peculiarities whatever; the way in which a person conducts himself in private relations, etc., and is not limited to his idiosyncrasy in its practical and active phase. I shall, therefore, use the term "passions"; understanding thereby the particular bent of character, as far as the peculiarities of volition are not limited to private interest, but supply the impelling and actuating force for accomplishing deeds shared in by the community at large. Passion is in the first instance the *subjective,* and therefore the *formal* side of energy, will, and activity – leaving the object or aim still undetermined. And there is a similar relation of formality to reality in merely individual conviction, individual views, individual conscience. It is always a question of essential importance, what is the purport of my conviction, what the object of my passion, in deciding whether the one or the other is of a true and substantial nature. Conversely, if it is so, it will inevitably attain actual existence – be realized.

From this comment on the second essential element in the historical embodiment of an aim, we infer – glancing at the institution of the State in passing – that a State is then well constituted and internally powerful, when the private interest of its citizens is one with the common interest of the State; when the one finds its gratification and realization in the other – a proposition in itself very important. But in a State many institutions must be adopted, much political machinery invented, accompanied by appropriate political arrangements – necessitating long struggles of the understanding before what is really appropriate can be discovered – involving, moreover, contentions with private interest and passions, and a tedious discipline of these latter, in order to bring about the desired harmony. The epoch when a State attains this harmonious conditon, marks the period of its bloom, its virtue, its vigor, and its prosperity. But the history of mankind does not begin with a *conscious* aim of any kind, as it is the case with the particular circles into which men form themselves of set purpose. The mere social instinct implies a conscious purpose of security for life and property; and when society has been constituted, this purpose becomes more comprehensive. The History of the World begins with its general aim – the realization of the Idea of Spirit – only in an *implicit* form (*an sich*) that is, as Nature; a hidden, most profoundly hidden, unconscious instinct; and the whole process of History (as already observed), is directed to rendering this unconscious impulse a conscious one. Thus appearing in the form of merely natural existence, natural will – that which has been called the subjective side – physical craving, instinct, passion, private interest, as also opinion and subjective conception – spontaneously present themselves at the very commencement. This vast congeries of volitions, interests and activities, constitute the instruments and means of the World- Spirit for attaining its object; bringing it to consciousness, and realizing it. And this aim is none other than finding itself – coming to itself – and contemplating itself in concrete actuality. But that those manifestations of vitality on the part of individuals and peoples, in which they seek and satisfy their own purposes, are, at the same time, the means and instruments of a higher and broader purpose of which they know nothing – which they realize unconsciously – might be made a matter of question; rather has been questioned, and in every variety of form negatived, decried and contemned as mere dreaming and "Philosophy." But on this point I announced my view at the very outset, and asserted our hypothesis – which, however, will appear in the sequel, in the form of a legitimate inference – and our belief that Reason governs the world, and has consequently governed its history. In relation to this independently universal and substantial existence – all else is subordinate, subservient to it, and the means for its development. – The Union of Universal Abstract Existence generally with the Individual – the

38

Subjective – that this alone is Truth, belongs to the department of speculation, and is treated in this general form in Logic. – But in the process of the World's History itself – as still incomplete – the abstract final aim of history is not yet made the distinct object of desire and interest. While these limited sentiments are still unconscious of the purpose they are fulfilling, the universal principle is implicit in them, and is realizing itself through them. The question also assumes the form of the union of *Freedom* and *Necessity;* the latent abstract process of Spirit being regarded as *Necessity,* while that which exhibits itself in the conscious will of men, as their interest, belongs to the domain of *Freedom.* As the metaphysical connection (*i.e.,* the connection in the Idea) of these forms of thought, belongs to Logic, it would be out of place to analyze it here. The chief and cardinal points only shall be mentioned.

Philosophy shows that the Idea advances to an infinite antithesis; that, viz., between the Idea in its free, universal form – in which it exists for itself – and the contrasted form of abstract introversion, reflection on itself, which is formal existence-for-self, personality, formal freedom, such as belongs to Spirit only. The universal Idea exists thus as the substantial totality of things on the one side, and as the abstract essence of free volition on the other side. This reflection of the mind on itself is individual self-consciousness – the polar opposite of the Idea in its general form, and therefore existing in absolute Limitation. This polar opposite is consequently limitation, particularization, for the universal absolute being; it is the side of its *definite existence;* the sphere of its formal reality, the sphere of the reverence paid to God. – To comprehend the absolute connection of this antithesis, is the profound task of metaphysics. This Limitation originates all forms of particularity of whatever kind. The formal volition (of which we have spoken) wills itself; desires to make its own personality valid in all that it purposes and does: even the pious individual wishes to be saved and happy. This pole of the antithesis, existing for itself, is – in contrast with the Absolute Universal Being – a special separate existence, taking cognizance of specialty only, and willing that alone. In short it plays its part in the region of mere phenomena. This is the sphere of particular purposes, in effecting which individuals exert themselves on behalf of their individuality – give it full play and objective realization. This is also the sphere of happiness and its opposite. He is happy who finds his condition suited to his special character, will, and fancy, and so enjoys himself in that condition. The History of the World is not the theatre of happiness. Periods of happiness are blank pages in it, for they are periods of harmony – periods when the antithesis is in abeyance. Reflection on self – the Freedom above described – is abstractly defined as the formal element of the activity of the absolute Idea. The realizing *activity* of which we have spoken is the middle term of the Syllogism, one of whose extremes is the Universal essence, the *Idea,* which reposes in the penetralia of Spirit; and the other, the complex of external things – objective matter. That activity is the medium by which the universal latent principle is translated into the domain of objectivity.

I will endeavor to make what has been said more vivid and clear by examples.

The building of a house is, in the first instance, a subjective aim and design. On the other hand we have, as means, the several substances required for the work – Iron, Wood, Stones.

The elements are made use of in working up this material: fire to melt the iron, wind to blow the fire, water to set wheels in motion, in order to cut the wood, etc. The result is, that the wind, which has helped to build the house, is shut out by the house; so also are the violence of rains and floods, and the destructive powers of fire, so far as the house is made fireproof. The stones and beams obey the law of gravity – press downward – and so high walls are carried up. Thus the elements are made use of in accordance with their nature, and yet to co-operate for a product, by which their operation is limited. Thus the passions of men are gratified; they develop themselves and their aims in accordance with their natural tendencies, and build up the edifice of human society; thus fortifying a position for Right and Order *against themselves.*

The connection of events above indicated, involves also the fact, that in history an additional result is commonly produced by human actions beyond that which they aim at and obtain – that which they immediately recognize and desire. They gratify their own interest; but something further is thereby accomplished, latent in the actions in question, though not present to their consciousness, and not included in their design. An analogous example is offered in the case of a man who, from a feeling of revenge – perhaps not an unjust one, but produced by injury on the other's part – burns that other man's house. A connection is immediately established between the deed itself and a train of circumstances not directly included in it, taken abstractedly. In itself it consisted in merely presenting a small flame to a small portion of a beam. Events not involved in that simple act follow of themselves. The part of the beam which was set fire to is connected with its remote portions; the beam itself is united with the woodwork of the house generally, and this with other houses; so that a wide conflagration, ensues, which destroys the goods and chattels of many other persons besides his against whom the act of revenge was first directed; perhaps even costs not a few men their lives. This lay neither in the deed abstractedly, nor in the design of the man who committed it. But the action has a further general bearing. In the design of the doer it was only revenge executed against an individual in the destruction of his property, but it is moreover a crime, and that involves punishment also. This may not have been present to the mind of the perpetrator, still less in his intention; but his deed itself, the general principles it calls into play, its substantial content entails it. By this example I wish only to impress on you the consideration, that in a simple act, something further may be implicated than lies in the intention and consciousness of the agent. The example before us involves, however, this additional consideration, that the substance of the act, consequently we may say the act itself, recoils upon the perpetrator – reacts upon him with destructive tendency. This union of the two extremes – the embodiment of a general idea in the form of direct reality, and the elevation of a speciality into connection with universal truth – is brought to pass, at first sight, under the conditions of an utter diversity of nature between the two, and an indifference of the one extreme towards the other. The aims which the agents set before them are limited and special; but it must be remarked that the agents themselves are intelligent thinking beings. The purport of their desires is interwoven with *general, essential* considerations of justice, good, duty, etc.; for mere desire – volition in its rough and savage forms – falls not within the scene and sphere of Universal History. Those general considerations, which form at the same time a norm for directing aims and actions, have a determinate purport; for such an abstraction as "good for its own sake," has no place in living reality. If men are to act, they must not only intend the Good, but must have decided for themselves whether this or that particular thing is a Good. What special course of action, however, is good or not, is determined, as regards the ordinary contingencies of private life, by the laws and customs of a State; and here no great difficulty is presented. Each individual has his position; he knows on the whole what a just, honorable course of conduct is. As to ordinary, private relations, the assertion that it is difficult to choose the right and good – the regarding it as the mark of an exalted morality to find difficulties and raise scruples on that score – may be set down to an evil or perverse will, which seeks to evade duties not in themselves of a perplexing nature; or, at any rate, to an idly reflective habit of mind – where a feeble will affords no sufficient exercise to the faculties – leaving them therefore to find occupation within themselves, and to expend themselves on moral self-adulation.

It is quite otherwise with the comprehensive relations that History has to do with. In this sphere are presented those momentous collisions between existing, acknowledged duties, laws, and rights, and those contingencies which are adverse to this fixed system; which assail and even destroy its foundations and existence; whose tenor may nevertheless seem good – on the large scale advantageous – yes, even indispensable and necessary. These contingencies realize themselves in History: they involve a general principle of a different order from that on which depends the *permanence* of a people or a State. This principle is an essential phase in the development of the *creating* Idea, of Truth striving and urging towards (consciousness of) itself. Historical men – *World-Historical Individuals* – are those in whose aims such a general principle lies.

Caesar, in danger of losing a position, not perhaps at that time of superiority, yet at least of equality with the others who were at the head of the State, and of succumbing to those who were just on the point of becoming his enemies – belongs essentially to this category. These enemies – who were at the same time pursuing *their* personal aims – had the form of the constitution, and the power conferred by an appearance of justice, on their side. Caesar was contending for the maintenance of his position, honor, and safety; and, since the power of his opponents included the sovereignty over the provinces of the Roman Empire, his victory secured for him the conquest of that entire Empire; and he thus became – though leaving the form of the constitution – the Autocrat of the State. That which secured for him the execution of a design, which in the first instance was of negative import – the Autocracy of Rome – was, however, at the same time an independently necessary feature in the history of Rome and of the world. It was not, then, his private gain merely, but an unconscious impulse that occasioned the accomplishment of that for which the time was ripe. Such are all great historical men – whose own particular aims involve those large issues which are the will of the World-Spirit. They may be called Heroes, inasmuch as they have derived their purposes and their vocation, not from the calm, regular course of things, sanctioned by the existing order; but from a concealed fount – one which has not attained to phenomenal, present existence – from that inner Spirit, still hidden beneath the surface, which, impinging on the outer world as on a shell, bursts it in pieces, because it is another kernel than that which belonged to the shell in question. They are men, therefore, who appear to draw the impulse of their life from themselves; and whose deeds have produced a condition of things and a complex of historical relations which appear to be only *their* interest, and *their* work. Such individuals had no consciousness of the general Idea they were unfolding, while prosecuting those aims of theirs; on the contrary, they were practical, political men. But at the same time they were thinking men, who had an insight into the requirements of the time – *what was ripe for development.* This was the very Truth for their age, for their world; the species next in order, so to speak, and which was already formed in the womb of time. It was theirs to know this nascent principle; the necessary, directly sequent step in progress, which their world was to take; to make this their aim, and to expend their energy in promoting it. World-historical men – the Heroes of an epoch – must, therefore, be recognized as its clear-sighted ones; *their* deeds, *their* words are the best of that time. Great men have formed purposes to satisfy themselves, not others. Whatever prudent designs and counsels they might have learned from others, would be the more limited and inconsistent features in their career; for it was they who best understood affairs; from whom *others* learned, and approved, or at least acquiesced in – their policy. For that Spirit which had taken this fresh step in history

43

is the inmost soul of all individuals; but in a state of unconsciousness which the great men in question aroused. Their fellows, therefore, follow these soul-leaders; for they feel the irresistible power of their own inner Spirit thus embodied. If we go on to cast a look at the fate of these World-Historical persons, whose vocation it was to be the agents of the World-Spirit – we shall find it to have been no happy one. They attained no calm enjoyment; their whole life was labor and trouble; their whole nature was nought else but their master-passion. When their object is attained they fall off like empty hulls from the kernel. They die early, like Alexander; they are murdered, like Caesar; transported to St. Helena, like Napoleon. This fearful consolation – that historical men have not enjoyed what is called happiness, and of which only private life (and this may be passed under very various external circumstances) is capable – this consolation those may draw from history, who stand in need of it; and it is craved by Envy – vexed at what is great and transcendant – striving, therefore, to depreciate it, and to find some flaw in it. Thus in modern times it has been demonstrated *ad nauseam* that princes are generally unhappy on their thrones; in consideration of which the possession of a throne is tolerated, and men acquiesce in the fact that not themselves but the personages in question are its occupants. The Free Man, we may observe, is not envious, but gladly recognizes what is great and exalted, and rejoices that it exists.

It is in the light of those common elements which constitute the interest and therefore the passions of individuals, that these historical men are to be regarded. They are *great* men, because they willed and accomplished something great; not a mere fancy, a mere intention, but that which met the case and fell in with the needs of the age. This mode of considering them also excludes the so-called "psychological" view, which – serving the purpose of envy most effectually – contrives so to refer all actions to the heart – to bring them under such a subjective aspect – as that their authors appear to have done everything under the impulse of some passion, mean or grand – some *morbid craving* – and on account of these passions and cravings to have been not moral men. Alexander of Macedon partly subdued Greece, and then Asia; therefore he was possessed by a *morbid craving* for conquest. He is alleged to have acted from a craving for fame, for conquest; and the proof that these were the impelling motives is that he did that which resulted in fame. What pedagogue has not demonstrated of Alexander the Great – of Julius Caesar – that they were instigated by such passions, and were consequently immoral men? – whence the conclusion immediately follows that he, the pedagogue, is a better man than they, because he has not such passions; a proof of which lies in the fact that he does not conquer Asia – vanquish Darius and Porus – but while he enjoys life himself, lets others enjoy it too. These psychologists are particularly fond of contemplating those peculiarities of great historical figures which appertain to them as private persons. Man must eat and drink; he sustains relations to friends and acquaintances; he has passing impulses and ebullitions of temper. "No man is a hero to his *valet-de-chambre*" is a well-known proverb; I have added – and Goethe repeated it ten years later – "but not because the former is no hero, but because the latter is a valet." He takes off the hero's boots, assists him to bed, knows that he prefers champagne, etc. Historical personages waited upon in historical literature by such psychological valets, come poorly off; they are brought down by these their attendants to a level with – or rather a few degrees below the level of – the morality of such exquisite discerners of spirits. The Thersites of Homer who abuses the kings is a standing figure for all times. Blows – that is beating with a solid cudgel – he does not get in every age, as in the Homeric one; but his envy, his egotism, is the thorn which he has to carry in his flesh; and the undying worm that gnaws him is the tormenting consideration that his excellent views and vituperations remain absolutely without result in the world. But our satisfaction at the fate of Thersitism also may have its sinister side.

A World-historical individual is not so unwise as to indulge a variety of wishes to divide his regards. He is devoted to the One Aim, regardless of all else. It is even possible that such men may treat other great, even sacred interests, inconsiderately; conduct which is indeed obnoxious to moral reprehension. But so mighty a form must trample down many an innocent flower – crush to pieces many an object in its path.

The special interest of passion is thus inseparable from the active development of a general principle: for it is from the special and determinate and from its negation, that the Universal results. Particularity contends with its like, and some loss is involved in the issue.

It is not the general idea that is implicated in opposition and combat, and that is exposed to danger. It remains in the background, untouched and uninjured. This may be called the *cunning of reason* – that it sets the passions to work for itself, while that which develops its existence through such impulsion pays the penalty, and suffers loss. For it is *phenomenal* being that is so treated, and of this part is of no value, part is positive and real. The particular is for the most part of too trifling value as compared with the general: individuals are sacrificed and abandoned. The Idea pays the penalty of determinate existence and of corruptibility, not from itself, but from the passions of individuals.

But though we might tolerate the idea that individuals, their desires and the gratification of them, are thus sacrificed, and their happiness given up to the empire of chance, to which it belongs; and that as a general rule, individuals come under the category of means to an ulterior end – there is one aspect of human individuality which we should hesitate to regard in that subordinate light, even in relation to the highest; since it is absolutely no subordinate element, but exists in those individuals as inherently eternal and divine. I mean *morality, ethics, religion.* Even when speaking of the realization of the great ideal aim by means of individuals, the *subjective* element in them – their interest and that of their cravings and impulses, their views and judgments, though exhibited as the merely formal side of their existence – was spoken of as having an infinite right to be consulted. The first idea that presents itself in speaking of *means* is that of something external to the object, and having no share in the object itself. But merely natural things – even the commonest lifeless objects – used as means, must be of such a kind as adapts them to their purpose; they must possess something in common with it. Human beings least of all sustain the bare external relation of mere means to the great ideal aim. Not only do they in the very act of realizing it, make it the occasion of satisfying personal desires, whose purport is diverse from that aim – but they share in that ideal aim itself; and are for that very reason objects of their own existence; not *formally* merely, as the world of living beings generally is – whose individual life is essentially subordinate to that of man, and is properly used *up* as an instrument. Men, on the contrary, are objects of existence to themselves, as regards the intrinsic import of the aim in question. To this order belongs that in them which we would exclude from the category of mere means – Morality, Ethics, Religion. That is to say, man is an object of existence in himself only in virtue of the Divine that is in him – that which was designated at the outset as *Reason;* which, in view of its activity and power of self-determination, was called *Freedom.* And we affirm – without entering at present on the proof of the assertion – that Religion, Morality, etc., have their foundation and source in that principle, and so are essentially elevated above all alien necessity and chance. And here we must remark that individuals, to the extent of their freedom, are responsible for the depravation and enfeeblement of morals and religion. This is the seal of the absolute and sublime destiny of man – that he knows what is good and what is evil; that his Destiny *is* his very ability to will either good or evil – in one word, that he is the subject of moral imputation, imputation not only of evil, but of good; and not only concerning this or that particular matter, and all that happens *ab extra,* but *also* the good and evil attaching to his individual freedom. The brute alone is simply innocent. It would, however, demand an extensive explanation – as extensive as the analysis of moral freedom itself – to preclude or obviate all the misunderstandings which the statement that what is called innocence imports the entire unconsciousness of evil – is wont to occasion.

In contemplating the fate which virtue, morality, even piety experience in history, we must not fall into the Litany of Lamentations, that the good and pious often – or for the most part – fare ill in the world, while the evil-disposed and wicked prosper. The term *prosperity* is used in a variety of meanings – riches, outward honor, and the like. But in speaking of something which in and for itself constitutes an aim of existence, that so-called well or ill-faring of these or those isolated individuals cannot be regarded as an essential element in the rational order of the universe. With more justice than happiness – or a fortunate environment for individuals – it is demanded of the grand aim of the world's existence, that it should foster, nay involve the execution and ratification of good, moral, righteous purposes. What makes men morally discontented (a discontent, by the bye, on which they somewhat pride themselves), is that they do not find the present adapted to the realization of aims which they hold to be right and just (more especially in modern times, ideals of political constitutions); they contrast unfavorably things as they *are,* with their idea of things as they *ought* to be. In this case it is not private interest nor passion that desires gratification, but Reason, Justice, Liberty; and equipped with this title, the demand in question assumes a lofty bearing, and readily adopts a position not merely of discontent, but of open revolt against the actual condition of the world. To estimate such a feeling and such views aright, the demands insisted upon, and the very dogmatic opinions asserted, must be examined. At no time so much as in our own, have such general principles and notions been advanced, or with greater assurance. If in days gone by, history seems to present itself as a struggle of passions; in our time – though displays of passion are not wanting – it exhibits partly a predominance of the struggle of notions assuming the authority of principles; partly that of passions and interests essentially subjective, but under the mask of such higher sanctions. The pretensions thus contended for as legitimate in the name of that which has been stated as the ultimate aim of Reason, pass accordingly, for absolute aims – to the same extent as Religion, Morals, Ethics. Nothing, as before remarked, is now more common than the complaint that the *ideals* which imagination sets up are not realized – that these glorious dreams are destroyed by cold actuality. These Ideals – which in the voyage of life founder on the rocks of hard reality – may be in the first instance only subjective, and belong to the idiosyncrasy of the individual, imagining himself the highest and wisest. Such do not properly belong to this category. For the fancies which the individual in his isolation indulges, cannot be the model for universal reality; just as *universal* law is not designed for the units of the mass. These as such may, in fact, find their interests decidedly thrust into the background. But by the term "Ideal," we also understand the ideal of Reason, of the Good, of the True. Poets, *e.g.,* Schiller, have painted such ideals touchingly and with strong emotion, and with the deeply melancholy conviction that they could not be realized. In affirming, on the contrary, that the Universal Reason *does* realize itself, we have indeed nothing to do with the individual empirically regarded. That admits of degrees of better and worse, since here chance and speciality have received authority from the Idea to exercise their monstrous power. Much, therefore, in particular aspects of the grand phenomenon might be found fault with. This subjective faultfinding – which, however, only keeps in view the individual and its deficiency, without taking notice of Reason pervading the whole – is easy; and inasmuch as it asserts an excellent intention with regard to the good of the whole, and seems to result from a kindly heart, it feels authorized to give itself airs and assume great consequence. It is easier to discover a deficiency in individuals, in states, and in Providence, than to see their real import and value. For in this merely negative faultfinding a proud position is taken – one which overlooks the object, without having entered into it – without having comprehended its positive aspect. Age generally makes men more tolerant; youth is always discontented. The tolerance of age is the result of the ripeness of a judgment which, not merely as the result of indifference, is satisfied even with what is inferior; but, more deeply taught by the grave experience of life, has been led to perceive the substantial, solid worth of the object in question. The insight then to which – in contradistinction from those ideals – philosophy is to lead us, is, that the real world is as it ought to be – that the truly good – the universal divine reason – is not a mere abstraction, but a vital principle capable of realizing itself. This *Good*, this *Reason*, in its most concrete form, is God. God governs the world; the actual working of his government – the carrying out of his plan – is the History of the World. This plan philosophy strives to comprehend; for only that which has been developed as the result of it, possesses *bond fide* reality. That which does not accord with it, is negative, worthless existence. Before the pure light of this divine Idea – which is no mere Ideal – the phantom of a world whose events are an incoherent concourse of fortuitous circumstances, utterly vanishes. Philosophy wishes to discover the substantial purport, the real side, of the divine idea, and to justify the so much despised Reality of things; for Reason is the comprehension of the Divine work. But as to what concerns the perversion, corruption, and ruin of religious, ethical, and moral purposes, and states of society generally, it must be affirmed that in their *essence* these are infinite and eternal; but that the forms they assume may be of a limited order, and consequently belong to the domain of mere nature, and be subject to the sway of chance. They are therefore perishable, and exposed to decay and corruption. Religion and morality – in the same way as inherently universal essences – have the peculiarity of being present in the individual soul, in the full extent of their Idea, and therefore truly and really; although, they may not manifest themselves in it *in extenso,* and are not applied to fully developed relations. The religion, the morality of a limited sphere of life – that of a shepherd or a peasant, *e.g.,* – in its intensive concentration and limitation to a few perfectly simple relations of life – has infinite worth; the same worth as the religion and morality of extensive knowledge, and of an existence rich in the compass of its relations and actions. This inner focus – this simple region of the claims of subjective freedom – the home of volition, resolution, and action – the abstract sphere of conscience – that which comprises the responsibility and moral value of the individual, remains untouched; and is quite shut out from the noisy din of the World's History – including not merely external and temporal changes, but also those entailed by the absolute necessity inseparable from the realization of the Idea of Freedom itself. But as a general truth this must be regarded as settled, that whatever in the world possesses claims as noble and glorious, has nevertheless a higher existence above it. The claim of the World-Spirit rises above all special claims. These observations may suffice in reference to the means which the World-Spirit uses for realizing its Idea. Stated simply and abstractly, this mediation involves the activity of personal existences in whom Reason is present as their absolute, substantial being; but a basis, in the first instance, still obscure and unknown to them. But the subject becomes more complicated and difficult when we regard individuals not merely in their aspect of activity, but more concretely, in conjunction with a particular manifestation of that activity in their religion and morality – forms of existence which are intimately connected with Reason, and share in its absolute claims. Here the relation of mere means to an end disappears, and the chief bearings of this seeming difficulty in reference to the absolute aim of Spirit have been briefly considered.

(3) The third point to be analyzed is, therefore – what is the object to be realized by these means; *i.e.* what is the form it assumes in the realm of reality. We have spoken of *means;* but in the carrying out of a subjective, limited aim, we have also to take into consideration the element of a *material,* either already present or which has to be procured. Thus the question would arise: What is the material in which the Ideal of Reason is wrought out? The primary answer would be – Personality itself – human desires – Subjectivity generally. In human knowledge and

volition, as its material element, Reason attains positive existence. We have considered subjective volition where it has an object which is the truth and essence of a reality, viz., where it constitutes a great world-historical passion. As a subjective will, occupied with limited passions, it is dependent, and can gratify its desires only within the limits of this dependence. But the subjective will has also a substantial life – a reality – in which it moves in the region of *essential* being, and has the essential itself as the object of its existence. This essential being is the union of the *subjective* with the *rational* Will: it is the moral Whole, the *State,* which is that form of reality in which the individual has and enjoys his freedom; but on the condition of his recognizing, believing in, and willing that which is common to the Whole. And this must not be understood as if the subjective will of the social unit attained its gratification and enjoyment through that common Will; as if this were a means provided for its benefit; as if the individual, in his relations to other individuals, thus limited his freedom, in order that this universal limitation – the mutual constraint of all – might secure a small space of liberty for each. Rather, we affirm, are Law, Morality, Government, and they alone, the positive reality and completion of Freedom. Freedom of a low and limited order is mere caprice; which finds its exercise in the sphere of particular and limited desires.

Subjective volition – Passion – is that which sets men in activity, that which effects "practical" realization. The Idea is the inner spring of action; the State is the actually existing, realized moral life. For it is the Unity of the universal, essential Will, with that of the individual; and this is "Morality." The Individual living in this unity has a moral life; possesses a value that consists in this substantiality alone. Sophocles in his Antigone, says, "The divine commands are not of yesterday, nor of today; no, they have an infinite existence, and no one could say whence they came." The laws of morality are not accidental, but are the essentially Rational. It is the very object of the State that what is essential in the practical activity of men, and in their dispositions, should be duly recognized; that it should have a manifest existence, and maintain its position. It is the absolute interest of Reason that this moral Whole should exist; and herein lie the justification and merit of heroes who have founded states – however rude these may have been. In the history

51

of the World, only those peoples can come under our notice which form a state. For it must be understood that this latter is the realization of Freedom, *i.e.,* of the absolute final aim, and that it exists for its own sake. It must further be understood that all the worth which the human being possesses – all spiritual reality, he possesses only through the State. For his spiritual reality consists in this, that his own essence – Reason – is objectively present to him, that it possesses objective immediate existence for him.

Thus only is he fully conscious; thus only is he a partaker of morality – of a just and moral social and political life. For Truth is the Unity of the universal and subjective Will; and the Universal is to be found in the State, in its laws, its universal and rational arrangements. The State is the Divine Idea as it exists on Earth. We have in it, therefore, the object of History in a more definite shape than before; that in which Freedom obtains objectivity, and lives in the enjoyment of this objectivity. For Law is the objectivity of Spirit; volition in its true form. Only that will which obeys law, is free: for it obeys itself – it is independent and so free. When the State or our country constitutes a community of existence; when the subjective will of man submits to laws – the contradiction between Liberty and Necessity vanishes. The Rational has necessary existence, as being the reality and substance of things, and we are free in recognizing it as law, and following it as the substance of our own being. The objective and the subjective will are then reconciled, and present one identical homogeneous whole. For the morality *(Sittlichkeit)* of the State is not of that ethical (*moralische*) reflective kind, in which one's own conviction bears sway; this latter is rather the peculiarity of the modern time, while the true antique morality is based on the principle of abiding by one's duty [to the state at large]. An Athenian citizen did what was required of him, as it were from instinct: but if I reflect on the object of my activity, I must have the consciousness that my will has been called into exercise. But morality is Duty – substantial Right – a *"second nature"* as it has been justly called; for the *first* nature of man is his primary merely animal existence.

The development *in extenso* of the Idea of the State belongs to the Philosophy of Jurisprudence; but it must be observed that in the theories of our time various errors are current respecting it, which pass for established truths, and have become fixed prejudices. We will mention only a few of them, giving prominence to such as have a reference to the object of our history.

The error which first meets us is the direct contradictory of our principle that the state presents the realization of Freedom; the opinion, viz., that man is free by *nature,* but that in *society,* in the State – to which nevertheless he is irresistibly impelled – he must limit this natural freedom. That man is free by Nature is quite correct in one sense; viz., that he is so according to the Idea of Humanity; but we imply thereby that he *is* such only in virtue of his destiny – that he has an undeveloped power to become such; for the "Nature" of an object is exactly synonymous with its "Idea." But the view in question imports more than this. When man is spoken of as "free by Nature," the mode of his existence as well as his destiny *is* implied. His merely natural and primary condition is intended. In this sense a "state of Nature" is assumed in which mankind at large are in the possession of their natural rights with the unconstrained exercise and enjoyment of their freedom. This assumption is not indeed raised to the dignity of the historical fact; it would indeed be difficult, were the attempt seriously made, to point out any such condition as actually existing, or as having ever occurred. Examples of a savage state of life can be pointed out, but they are marked by brutal passions and deeds of violence; while, however rude and simple their conditions, they involve social arrangements which (to use the common phrase) *restrain* freedom. That assumption is one of those nebulous images which theory produces; an idea which it cannot avoid originating, but which it fathers upon real existence, without sufficient historical justification.

What we find such a state of Nature to be in actual experience, answers exactly to the Idea of a *merely* natural condition.

Freedom as the *ideal* of that which is original and natural, does not exist *as original and natural.* Rather must it be first sought out and won; and that by an incalculable medial discipline ' of the intellectual and moral powers. The state of Nature is, therefore, predominantly that of injustice and violence, of untamed natural impulses, of inhuman deeds and feelings. Limitation is certainly produced by Society and the State, but it is a limitation of the mere brute emotions and rude instincts; as also, in a more advanced stage of culture, of the premeditated self-will of caprice and passion. This kind of constraint is part of the instrumentality by which only, the consciousness of Freedom and the desire for its attainment, in its true – that is Rational and Ideal form – can be obtained. To the Ideal of Freedom, Law and Morality are indispensably requisite; and they are in and for themselves, universal existences, objects and aims; which are discovered only by the activity of thought, separating itself from the merely sensuous, and developing itself, in opposition thereto; and which must on the other hand, be introduced into and incorporated with the originally sensuous will, and that contrarily to its natural inclination. The perpetually recurring misapprehension of Freedom consists in regarding that term only in its *formal,* subjective sense, abstracted from its essential objects and aims; thus a constraint put upon impulse, desire, passion – pertaining to the particular individual as such – a limitation of caprice and self-will is regarded as a fettering of Freedom. We should on the contrary look upon such limitation as the indispensable proviso of emancipation. Society and the State are the very conditions in which Freedom is realized. We must notice a second view, contravening the principle of the development of moral relations into a legal form. The *patriarchal* condition is regarded – either in reference to the entire race of man, or to some branches of it – as exclusively that condition of things, in which the legal element is combined with a due recognition of the moral and emotional parts of our nature; and in which justice as united with these, truly and really influences the intercourse of the social units. The basis of the patriarchal condition is the family relation; which develops the *primary* form of conscious morality, succeeded by that of the State as its *second* phase. The patriarchal condition is one of transition, in which the family has already advanced to the position of a race or people; where the union, therefore, has already ceased to be simply a bond of love and confidence, and has become one of plighted service. We must first examine the ethical principle of the Family. The Family may be reckoned as virtually a single person; since its members have either mutually surrendered their individual personality, (and consequently their legal position towards each other, with the rest of their particular interests and desires) as in the case of the Parents; or have not yet attained such an independent

54

personality – (the Children – who are primarily in that merely natural condition already mentioned). They live, therefore, in a unity of feeling, love, confidence, and faith in each other. And in a relation of natural love, the one individual has the consciousness of himself in the consciousness of the other; he lives out of self; and in this mutual self-renunciation each regains the life that had been virtually transferred to the other; gains, in fact, that other's existence and his own, as involved with that other. The farther interests connected with the necessities and external concerns of life, as well as the development that has to take place within their circle, *i.e.,* of the children, constitute a common object for the members of the Family. The Spirit of the Family – the Penates – form one substantial being, as much as the Spirit of a People in the State; and morality in both cases consists in a feeling, a consciousness, and a will, not limited to individual personality and interest, but embracing the common interests of the members generally. But this unity is in the case of the Family essentially one of *feeling;* not advancing beyond the limits of the merely *natural.* The piety of the Family relation should be respected in the highest degree by the State; by its means the State obtains as its members individuals who are already moral (for as mere *persons* they are not) and who in uniting to form a state bring with them that sound basis of a political edifice – the capacity of feeling one with a Whole. But the expansion of the Family to a patriarchal unity carries us beyond the ties of blood-relationship – the simply natural elements of that basis; and outside of these limits the members of the community must enter upon the position of independent personality. A review of the patriarchal condition, *in extenso,* would lead us to give special attention to the Theocratical Constitution. The head of the patriarchal clan is also its priest. If the Family in its general relations, is not yet separated from civic society and the state, the separation of religion from it has also not yet taken place; and so much the less since the piety of the hearth is itself a profoundly subjective state of feeling.

We have considered two aspects of Freedom, – the objective and the subjective; if, therefore, Freedom is asserted to consist in the individuals of a State all agreeing in its arrangements, it *is* evident that only the subjective aspect is regarded. The natural inference from this principle is, that no law can be valid without the approval of all. This difficulty is attempted to be obviated by the decision that the minority must yield to the majority; the majority therefore bear the sway. But long ago J. J. Rousseau remarked that in that case there would be no longer freedom, for the will of the *minority* would cease to be respected. At the Polish Diet each single member had to give his consent before any political step could be taken; and this kind of freedom it was that ruined the State. Besides, it is a dangerous and false prejudice, that the People *alone* have reason and insight, and know what justice is; for each popular faction may represent itself as the People, and the question as to what constitutes the State is one of advanced science, and not of popular decision. If the principle of regard for the individual will is recognized as the only basis of political liberty, viz., that nothing should be done by or for the State to which all the members of the body politic have not given their sanction, we have, properly speaking, no *Constitution.* The only arrangement that would be necessary, would be, first, a centre having no *will* of its own, but which should take into consideration what appeared to be the necessities of the State; and, secondly, a contrivance for calling the members of the State together, for taking the votes, and for performing the arithmetical operations of reckoning and comparing the number of votes for the different propositions, and thereby deciding upon them. The State is an *abstraction,* having even its generic existence in its citizens; but it is an actuality, and its simply generic existence must embody itself in individual will and activity. The want of government and political administration in general is felt; this necessitates the selection and separation from the rest of those who have to take the helm in political affairs, to decide concerning them, and to give orders to other citizens, with a view to the execution of their plans. If *e.g.,* even the people in a Democracy resolve on a war, a general must head the army. It is only by a Constitution that the *abstraction* – the State – attains life and reality; but this involves the distinction between those who command and those who obey. – Yet obedience seems inconsistent with liberty, and those who command appear to do the very opposite of that which the fundamental idea of the State, viz. that of Freedom, requires. It is, however, urged that – though the distinction between commanding and obeying is absolutely necessary, because affairs could not go on without it – and indeed this seems only a compulsory limitation, external to and even contravening freedom in the abstract – the constitution should be at least so framed, that the citizens may obey as little as possible, and the smallest modicum of free volition be left to the commands of the superiors; – that the substance of that for which subordination is necessary, even in its most important bearings, should be decided and resolved on by the People – by the will of many or of all the citizens; though it is supposed to be thereby provided that the State should be possessed of vigor and strength as a reality – an individual unity. – The primary consideration is, then, the distinction between the governing and the governed, and the political constitutions in the abstract have been rightly divided into Monarchy, Aristocracy, and Democracy; which gives occasion, however, to the remark that Monarchy itself must be further divided into Despotism and Monarchy proper; that in all the divisions to which the leading Idea gives rise, only the generic character is to be made prominent – it being not intended thereby that the particular category under review should be exhausted as a Form, Order, or Kind in its *concrete* development. But especially it must be observed, that the abovementioned divisions admit of a multitude of particular modifications – not only such as lie within the limits of those classes themselves – but also such as are mixtures of several of these essentially distinct classes, and which are consequently misshapen, unstable, and inconsistent forms. In such a collision, the concerning question is, what is the *best constitution;* that is, by what arrangement, organization, or mechanism of the power of the State its object can be most surely attained. This object may indeed be variously understood; for instance, as the calm enjoyment of life on the part of the citizens, or as Universal Happiness. Such aims have suggested the so-called Ideals of Constitutions, and – as a particular branch of the subject – Ideals of the Education of Princes (Fenelon), or of the governing body – the aristocracy at large (Plato); for the chief point they treat of is the condition of those subjects who stand at the head of affairs: and in these Ideals the concrete details of political organization are not at all considered. The inquiry into the best constitution is frequently treated *as* if not only the theory were an affair of subjective independent conviction, but as if the introduction of a constitution recognized as the best – or *as* superior to others – could be the result of a resolve adopted in this theoretical manner; as if the form of a constitution were a matter of free choice, determined by nothing else but reflection. Of this artless fashion was that deliberation – not indeed of the Persian *people,* but of the Persian *grandees,* who had conspired to overthrow the pseudo-Smerdis and the Magi, after their undertaking had succeeded, and when there was no scion of the royal family living – as to what constitution they should introduce into Persia; and Herodotus gives an equally naive account of this deliberation.

In the present day, the Constitution of a country and people is not represented as so entirely dependent on free and deliberate choice. The fundamental but abstractly (and therefore imperfectly) entertained conception of Freedom, has resulted in the Republic being very generally regarded – in *theory* – as the only just and true political constitution. Many even, who occupy elevated official positions under monarchical constitutions – so far from being opposed to this idea – are actually its supporters; only they see that such a constitution, though the best, cannot be realized under all circumstances; and that – while men are what they are – we must be satisfied with less if freedom; the monarchical constitution – under the given circumstances, and the present moral condition of the people – being even regarded as the most advantageous. In this view also, the necessity of a particular constitution is made to depend on the condition of the people in such a way *as* if the latter were non-essential and accidental. This representation is founded on the distinction which the reflective understanding makes between an idea and the corresponding reality; holding to an abstract and consequently untrue idea; not grasping it in its completeness, or – which is virtually, though not in point of form, the same – not taking a concrete view of a people and a state. We shall have to show further on that the constitution adopted by a people makes one substance – one spirit: – with its religion, its art and philosophy, or, at least, with its conceptions and thoughts – its culture generally; not to expatiate upon the additional influences, *ab extra,* of climate, of neighbors, of its place in the World. A State is an individual totality, of which you cannot select any particular side, although a supremely important one, such as its political constitution; and deliberate and decide respecting it in that isolated form. Not only is that constitution most intimately connected with and dependent on those other spiritual forces; but the form of the entire moral and intellectual individuality – comprising all the forces it embodies – is only a step in the development of the grand Whole – with its place pre-appointed in the process; a fact which gives the highest sanction to the constitution in question, and establishes its absolute necessity. – The origin of a state involves imperious lordship on the one hand, instinctive submission on the other. But even obedience – lordly power, and the fear inspired by a ruler – in itself implies some degree of voluntary connection. Even in barbarous states this is the case; it is not the isolated will of individuals that prevails; individual pretensions are relinquished, and the general will is the essential bond of political union. This unity of the general and the particular is the Idea itself, manifesting itself as a *state,* and which subsequently undergoes further development within itself. The abstract yet necessitated process in the development of truly independent states is as follows: – They begin with regal power, whether of patriarchal or military origin. In the next phase, particularity and individuality assert themselves in the form of Aristocracy and Democracy. Lastly, we have the subjection of these separate interests to a single power; but which can be absolutely none other than one outside of which those spheres have an independent position, viz., the Monarchical. Two phases of royalty, therefore, must be distinguished – a primary and a secondary one. This process *is* necessitated, so that the form of government assigned to a particular stage of development *must* present itself: it is therefore no matter of choice, but is that form which is adapted to the spirit of the people.

In a Constitution the main feature of interest is the self-development of the *rational,* that is, the *political* condition of a people; the setting free of the successive elements of the Idea: so that the several powers in the State manifest themselves as separate – attain their appropriate and special perfection – and yet in this independent condition, work together for one object, and are held together by it – *i.e.,* form an organic whole. The State is thus the embodiment of rational freedom, realizing and recognizing itself in an objective form. For its objectivity consists in this – that its successive stages are not merely ideal, but are present in an appropriate reality; and that in their separate and several working, they are absolutely merged in that agency by which the totality – the soul – the individuate unity – is produced, and of which it is the result.

The State is the Idea of Spirit in the external manifestation of human Will and its Freedom. It is to the State, therefore, that change in the aspect of History indissolubly attaches itself; and the successive phases of the Idea manifest themselves in it as distinct political *principles.* The Constitutions under which World-Historical peoples have reached their culmination, are peculiar to them; and therefore do not present a generally applicable political basis. Were it otherwise, the differences of similar constitutions would consist only in a peculiar method of expanding and developing that generic basis; whereas they really originate in diversity of principle. From the comparison therefore of the political institutions of the ancient World-Historical peoples, it so happens, that for the most recent principle of a Constitution – for the principle of our own times – nothing (so to speak) can be learned. In science and art it is quite otherwise; *e.g.,* the ancient philosophy is so decidedly the basis of the modern, that it is inevitably contained in the latter, and constitutes its basis. In this case the relation is that of a continuous development of the same structure, whose foundation-stone, walls, and roof have remained what they were. In Art, the Greek itself, in its original form, furnishes us the best models. But in regard to political constitution, it is quite otherwise : here the Ancient and the Modern have not their essential principle in common. Abstract definitions and dogmas respecting just government – importing that intelligence and virtue ought to bear sway – are, indeed, common to both. But nothing is so absurd as to look to Greeks, Romans, or Orientals, for models for the political arrangements of our time. From the East may be derived beautiful pictures of a patriarchal condition, of paternal government, and of devotion to it on the part of peoples; from Greeks and Romans, descriptions of popular liberty. Among the latter we find the idea of a Free Constitution admitting all the citizens to a share in deliberations and resolves respecting the affairs and laws of the Commonwealth. In our times, too, this is its general acceptation; only with this modification, that – since our states are so large, and there are so many of "the Many," the latter – direct action being impossible – should by the indirect method of elective substitution express their concurrence with resolves affecting the common weal; that is, that for legislative purposes generally, the people should be represented by deputies. The so-called Representative Constitution is that form of government with which we connect the idea of a free constitution; and this notion has become a rooted prejudice. On this theory People and Government are separated. But there is a perversity in this antithesis; an ill-intentioned *ruse* designed to insinuate that the People are the totality of the State. Besides, the basis of this view is the principle of isolated individuality – the absolute validity of the subjective will – a dogma which we have already investigated. The great point is, that Freedom in its Ideal conception has not subjective will and caprice for its principle, but the recognition of the universal will; and that the process by which Freedom is realized is the free development of its successive stages. The subjective will is a merely formal determination – a *carte blanche* – not including what it is that is willed. Only the *rational* will is that universal principle which independently determines and unfolds its own being, and develops its successive elemental phases as organic members. Of this Gothic-cathedral architecture the ancients knew nothing. At an earlier stage of the discussion we established the two elemental considerations: first, the *idea* of freedom as the absolute and final aim; secondly, the *means* for realizing it, *i.e.,* the subjective side of knowledge and will, with its life, movement, and activity. We then recognized the State as the moral Whole and the Reality of Freedom, and consequently as the objective unity of these two elements. For although we make this distinction into two aspects for our consideration, it must be remarked that they are intimately connected; and that their connection is involved in the idea of each when examined separately. We have, on the one hand, recognized the Idea in the definite form of Freedom conscious of and willing itself – having itself alone as its object: involving at the same time, the pure and simple Idea of Reason, and likewise, that which we have called subject – self-consciousness – Spirit actually existing in the World. If, on the other hand, we consider Subjectivity, we find that subjective knowledge and will is Thought. But by the very act of thoughtful cognition and volition, I will the universal object – the substance of absolute Reason. We observe, therefore, an essential union between the objective side – the Idea – and the subjective side – the personality that conceives and wills it. – The *objective* existence of this union is the State, which is therefore the basis and centre of the other concrete elements of the life of a people – of Art, of Law, of Morals, of Religion, of Science. All the activity of Spirit has only this object – the becoming conscious of this union, *i.e.,* of its own Freedom. Among the

61

forms of this conscious union *Religion* occupies the highest position. In it, Spirit – rising above the limitations of temporal and secular existence – becomes conscious of the Absolute Spirit, and in this consciousness of the self-existent Being, renounces its individual interest; it lays this aside in Devotion – a state of mind in which it refuses to occupy itself any longer with the limited and particular. By Sacrifice man expresses his renunciation of his property, his will, his individual feelings. The religious concentration of the soul appears in the form of feeling; it nevertheless passes also into reflection; a form of worship (*cultus*) is a result of reflection. The second form of the union of the objective and subjective in the human spirit is *Art.* This advances farther into the realm of the actual and sensuous than Religion. In its noblest walk it is occupied with representing, not indeed, the Spirit of God, but certainly the Form of God; and in its secondary aims, that which is divine and spiritual generally. Its office is to render visible the Divine; presenting it to the imaginative and intuitive faculty. But the True is the object not only of conception and feeling, as in Religion – and of intuition, as in Art – but also of the thinking faculty; and this gives us the third form of the union in question – *Philosophy.* This is consequently the highest, freest, and wisest phase. Of course we are not intending to investigate these three phases here; they have only suggested themselves in virtue of their occupying the same general ground as the object here considered – the *State.*

The general principle which manifests itself and becomes an object of consciousness in the State – the form under which all that the State includes is brought – is the whole of that cycle of phenomena which constitutes the *culture* of a nation. But the definite *substance* that receives the form of universality, and exists in that concrete reality which is the State – is the Spirit of the People itself. The actual State is animated by this spirit, in all its particular affairs – its Wars, Institutions, etc. But man must also attain a conscious realization of this his Spirit and essential nature, and of his original identity with it. For we said that morality is the identity of the *subjective* or *personal* with the *universal* will. Now the mind must give itself an express consciousness of this; and the focus of this knowledge is *Religion.* Art and Science are only various aspects and forms of the same substantial being. – In considering

Religion, the chief point of inquiry is, whether it recognizes the True – the Idea – only in its separate, abstract form, or in its true unity; in *separation* – God being represented in an abstract form as the Highest Being, Lord of Heaven and Earth, living in a remote region far from human actualities – or in its *unity* – God, as Unity of the Universal and Individual; the Individual itself assuming the aspect of positive and real existence in the idea of the Incarnation. Religion is the sphere in which a nation gives itself the definition of that which it regards as the True. A definition contains everything that belongs to the essence of an object; reducing its nature to its simple characteristic predicate, as a mirror for every predicate – the generic soul pervading all its details. The conception of God, therefore, constitutes the general basis of a people's character.

In this aspect, religion stands in the closest connection with the political principle. Freedom can exist only where Individuality is recognized as having its positive and real existence in the Divine Being. The connection may be further explained thus: – Secular existence, as merely temporal – occupied with particular interests – is consequently only relative and unauthorized; and receives its validity only in as far as the universal soul that pervades it – its principle – receives absolute validity; which it cannot have unless it is recognized as the definite manifestation, the phenomenal existence of the Divine Essence. On this account it is that the State rests on Religion. We hear this often repeated in our times, though for the most part nothing further is meant than that individual subjects as God-fearing men would be more disposed and ready to perform their duty; since obedience to King and Law so naturally follows in the train of reverence for God. This reverence, indeed, since it exalts the general over the special, may even turn upon the latter – become fanatical – and work with incendiary and destructive violence against the State, its institutions, and arrangements. Religious feeling, therefore, it is thought, should be sober – kept in a certain degree of coolness – that it may not storm against and bear down that which should be defended and preserved by it. The possibility of such a catastrophe is at least latent in it.

While, however, the correct sentiment is adopted, that the State is based on Religion, the position thus assigned to Religion supposes the State already to exist; and that subsequently, in order to maintain it, Religion must be brought into it – in buckets and bushels as it were – and impressed upon people's hearts. It is quite true that men must be trained to religion, but not as to something whose existence has yet to begin. For in affirming that the State is based on Religion – that it has its roots in it – we virtually assert that the former has proceeded from the latter; and that this derivation is going on now and will always continue; *i.e.,* the principles of the State must be regarded as valid in and for themselves, which can only be in so far as they are recognized as determinate manifestations of the Divine Nature. The form of Religion, therefore, decides that of the State and its constitution. The latter actually originated in the particular religion adopted by the nation; so that, in fact, the Athenian or the Roman State was possible only in connection with the specific form of Heathenism existing among the respective peoples; just as a Catholic State has a spirit and constitution different from that of a Protestant one.

If that outcry – that urging and striving for the implantation of Religion in the community – were an utterance of anguish and a call for help, as it often seems to be, expressing the danger of religion having vanished, or being about to vanish entirely from the State – that would be fearful indeed – worse, in fact, than this outcry supposes; for it implies the belief in a resource against the evil, viz., the implantation and inculcation of religion; whereas religion is by no means a thing to be so produced; its *self-production* (and there can be no other) lies much deeper. Another and opposite folly which we meet with in our time, is that of pretending to invent and carry out political constitutions independently of religion. The Catholic confession, although sharing the Christian name with the Protestant, does not concede to the State an inherent Justice and Morality – a concession which in the Protestant principle is fundamental. This tearing away of the political morality of the Constitution from its natural connection, is necessary to the genius of that religion, inasmuch as it does not recognize Justice and Morality as independent and substantial. But thus excluded from intrinsic worth – torn away from their last refuge – the sanctuary of conscience – the calm retreat where religion has its abode – the principles and institutions of political legislation are destitute of a real centre, to the same degree as they are compelled to remain abstract and indefinite.

Summing up what has been said of the State, we find that we have been led to call its vital principle, as actuating the individuals who compose it – Morality. The State, its laws, its arrangements, constitute the rights of its members; its natural features, its mountains, air, and waters, are *their* country, their fatherland, their outward material property; the history of this State, *their* deeds; what their ancestors have produced belongs to them and lives in their memory. All is their possession, just as they are possessed by it; for it constitutes their existence, their being. Their imagination is occupied with the ideas thus presented, while the adoption of these laws, and of a fatherland so conditioned is the expression of their will. It is this matured totality which thus constitutes *one* Being, the spirit of *one* People. To it the individual members belong; each unit is the Son of his Nation, and at the same time – in as far as the State to which he belongs is undergoing development – the Son of his Age. None remains behind it, still less advances beyond it. This spiritual Being (the Spirit of his Time) is his; he is a representative of it; it is that in which he originated, and in which he lives. Among the Athenians the word Athens had a double import; suggesting primarily a complex of political institutions, but no less, in the second place, that Goddess who represented the Spirit of the People and its unity.

This Spirit of a People is a *determinate* and particular Spirit, and is, as just stated, further modified by the degree of its historical development. This Spirit, then, constitutes the basis and substance of those other forms of a nation's consciousness, which have been noticed. For Spirit in its self-consciousness must become an object of contemplation to itself, and objectivity involves, in the first instance, the rise of differences which make up a total of distinct spheres of objective spirit; in the same way as the Soul exists only as the complex of its faculties, which in their form of concentration in a simple unity produce that Soul. It is thus *One Individuality* which, presented in its essence as God, is honored and enjoyed in *Religion*, which is exhibited as an object of sensuous contemplation in *Art*, and is apprehended as an intellectual conception, in *Philosophy*. In virtue of the original identity of their essence, purport, and object, these various forms are inseparably united with the Spirit of the State. Only in connection with this particular religion, can this particular political constitution exist; just as in such or such a State, such or such a Philosophy or order of Art.

The remark next in order is, that each particular National genius is to be treated as only One Individual in the process of Universal History. For that history is the exhibition of the divine, absolute development of Spirit in its highest forms – that gradation by which it attains its truth and consciousness of itself. The forms which these grades of progress assume are the characteristic "National Spirits" of History; the peculiar tenor of their moral life, of their Government, their Art, Religion, and Science. To realize these grades is the boundless impulse of the World-Spirit – the goal of its irresistible urging; for this division into organic members, and the full development of each, is its Idea. – Universal History is exclusively occupied with showing how Spirit comes to a recognition and adoption of the Truth: the dawn of knowledge appears; it begins to discover salient principles, and at last it arrives at full consciousness. Having, therefore, learned the abstract characteristics of the nature of Spirit, the means which it uses to realize its Idea, and the shape assumed by it in its complete realization in phenomenal existence – namely, the State – nothing further remains for this introductory section to contemplate but III. *The course of the World's History.* – The mutations which history presents have been long characterized in the general, as an advance to something better, more perfect. The changes that take place in Nature – how infinitely manifold soever they may be – exhibit only a perpetually self-repeating cycle; in Nature there happens "nothing new under the sun," and the multiform play of its phenomena so far induces a feeling of *ennui;* only in those changes which take place in the region of Spirit does anything new arise. This peculiarity in the world of mind has indicated in the case of man an altogether different destiny from that of merely natural objects – in which we find always one and the same stable character, to which all change reverts; – namely, a *real* capacity for change, and that for the better – an impulse of *perfectibility.* This principle, which reduces change itself under a law, has met with an unfavorable reception from religions – such as the Catholic – and from States claiming as their just right a stereotyped, or at least a stable position. If the mutability of worldly things in general – political constitutions, for instance – is conceded, either Religion (as the Religion of *Truth*) is absolutely excepted, or the difficulty escaped by ascribing changes, revolutions, and abrogations of immaculate theories and institutions, to accidents or imprudence – but principally to the levity and evil passions of man. The principle of Perfectibility indeed is almost as indefinite a term as mutability in general; it is without scope or goal, and has no standard by which to estimate the changes in question: the improved, more perfect, state of things towards which it professedly tends is altogether undetermined.

The principle of *Development* involves also the existence of a latent germ of being – a capacity or potentiality striving to realize itself. This formal conception finds actual existence in Spirit; which has the History of the World for its theatre, its possession, and the sphere of its realization. It is not of such a nature as to be tossed to and fro amid the superficial play of accidents, but is rather the absolute arbiter of things; entirely unmoved by contingencies, which, indeed, it applies and manages for its own purposes. Development, however, is also a property of organized natural objects. Their existence presents itself, not as an exclusively dependent one, subjected to external changes, but as one which expands itself in virtue of an internal unchangeable principle; a simple essence – whose existence, *i.e.,* as a germ, is primarily simple – but which subsequently develops a variety of parts, that become involved with other objects, and consequently live through a continuous process of changes; – a process nevertheless, that results in the very contrary of change, and is even transformed into a *vis conservatrix* of the organic principle, and the form embodying it. Thus the organized *individuum* produces itself; it expands itself *actually* to what it was always *potentially*. – So Spirit is only that which it attains by its own efforts; it makes itself *actually* what it always was *potentially*. – That development (of *natural organisms)* takes place in a direct, unopposed, unhindered manner. Between the Idea and its realization – the essential constitution of the original germ and the conformity to it of the existence derived from it – no disturbing influence can intrude. But in relation to Spirit it is quite otherwise. The realization of *its* Idea is mediated by consciousness and will; these very faculties are, in the first instance, sunk in their primary *merely* natural life; the first object and goal of their striving is the realization of their merely natural destiny – but which, since it is Spirit that animates it, is possessed of vast attractions and displays great power and (moral) richness. Thus Spirit is at war with itself; it has to overcome itself as its most formidable obstacle. That development which in the sphere of Nature is a peaceful growth is, in that of spirit, a severe, a mighty conflict with itself. What Spirit really strives for is the realization of its Ideal being; but in doing so, it hides that goal from its own vision, and is proud and well satisfied in this alienation from it.

Its expansion, therefore, does not present the harmless tranquillity of mere growth, as does that of organic life, but a stern reluctant working against itself. It exhibits, moreover, not the mere formal conception of development, but the attainment of a definite result. The goal of attainment we determined at the outset: it is Spirit in its *Completeness,* in its essential nature, *i.e.,* Freedom. This is the fundamental object, and therefore also the leading principle of the development – that whereby it receives meaning and importance (as in the Roman history, Rome is the object – consequently that which directs our consideration of the facts related); as, conversely, the phenomena of the process have resulted from this principle alone, and only as referred to it, possess a sense of value. There are many considerable periods in History in which this development seems to have been intermitted; in which, we might rather say, the whole enormous gain of previous culture appears to have been entirely lost; after which, unhappily, a new commencement has been necessary, made in the hope of recovering – by the assistance of some remains saved from the wreck of a former civilization, and by dint of a renewed incalculable expenditure of strength and time – one of the regions which had been an ancient possession of that civilization. We behold also *continued* processes of growth; structures and systems of culture in particular spheres, rich in kind, and well developed in every direction. The merely formal and indeterminate view of development in general can neither assign to one form of expansion superiority over the other, nor render comprehensible the object of that decay of older periods of growth; but must regard such occurrences – or, to speak more particularly, the retrocessions they exhibit – as external contingencies; and can only judge of particular modes of development from indeterminate points of view; which – since the development, as such, is all in all – are relative and not absolute goals of attainment.

Universal History exhibits the *gradation* in the development of that principle whose substantial *purport* is the consciousness of Freedom. The analysis of the successive grades, in their abstract form, belongs to Logic; in their concrete aspect to the Philosophy of Spirit. Here it is sufficient to state that the first step in the process presents that immersion of Spirit in Nature which has been already referred to; the second shows it as advancing to the consciousness of its freedom. But this initial separation from Nature is imperfect and partial, since it is derived immediately from the merely natural state, is consequently related to it, and is still encumbered with it as an essentially connected element. The third step is the elevation of the soul from this still limited and special form of freedom to its pure universal form; that state in which the spiritual essence attains the consciousness and feeling of itself. These grades are the ground-principles of the general process; but how each of them on the other hand involves within *itself* a process of formation – constituting the links in a dialectic of transition – to particularize this must be reserved for the sequel.

Here we have only to indicate that Spirit begins with a germ of infinite possibility, but *only* possibility – containing its substantial existence in an undeveloped form, as the object and goal which it reaches only in its resultant – full reality. In actual existence Progress appears as an advancing from the imperfect to the more perfect; but the former must not be understood abstractly as *only* the imperfect, but as something which involves the very opposite of itself – the so-called perfect – as a *germ* or impulse. So – reflectively, at least – *possibility* points to something destined to become actual; the Aristotelian δυναμισ is also *potentia,* power and might. Thus the Imperfect, as involving its opposite, is a contradiction, which certainly exists, but which is continually annulled and solved; the instinctive movement – the inherent impulse in the life of the soul – to break through the rind of mere nature, sensuousness, and that which is alien to it, and to attain to the light of consciousness, *i.e.,* to itself. We have already made the remark how the commencement' of the history of Spirit must be conceived so as to be in harmony with its Idea – in its bearing on the representations that have been made of a primitive "*natural* condition," in which freedom and justice are supposed to exist, or to have existed. This was, however, nothing more than an assumption of historical existence, conceived in the twilight of theorizing reflection. A pretension of quite another order – not a mere inference of reasoning, but making the claim of historical fact, and that supernaturally confirmed – is put forth in connection with a different view that is now widely promulgated by a certain class of speculatists. This view takes up the idea of the primitive paradisiacal conditon of man, which had been previously expanded by the Theologians, after their fashion – involving, *e.g.,* the supposition that God spoke with Adam in Hebrew – but remodelled to suit other requirements. The high authority appealed to in the first instance is the biblical narrative. But this depicts the primitive condition, partly only in the few wellknown traits, but partly either as in man generically – human nature at large – or, so far as Adam is to be taken as an individual, and consequently one person – as existing and completed in *this one,* or *only in one* human pair. The biblical account by no means justifies us in imagining a *people,* and a historical condition of such people, existing in that primitive form; still less does it warrant us in attributing to them the possession of a perfectly developed knowledge of God and Nature. "Nature," so the fiction runs, "like a clear mirror of God's creation, had originally lain revealed and transparent to the unclouded eye of man."[3] Divine Truth is imagined to have been equally manifest. It is even hinted, though left in some degree of obscurity, that in this primary condition men were in possession of an indefinitely extended and already expanded body of religious truths immediately revealed by God. This theory affirms that all religions had their historical commencement in this primitive knowledge, and that they polluted and obscured the original Truth by the monstrous creations of error and depravity; though in all the mythologies invented by Error, traces of that origin and of those primitive true dogmas are supposed to be present and cognizable. An important interest, therefore, accrues to the investigation of the history of ancient peoples, that, viz., of the endeavor to trace their annals up to the point where such fragments of the primary revelation are to be met with in greater purity than lower down.[4]

We owe to the interest which has occasioned these investigations, very much that is valuable; but this investigation bears direct testimony against itself, for it would seem to be awaiting the issue of an historical demonstration of that which is presupposed by it as historically established. That advanced condition of the knowledge of God, and of other scientific, *e.g.,* astronomical, knowledge (such as has been falsely attributed to the Hindoos); and the assertion that such a condition occurred at the very beginning of History – or that the religions of various nations were traditionally derived from it, and have developed themselves in degeneracy and depravation (as is represented in the rudely-conceived so-called "Emanation System"); – all these are suppositions which neither have, nor – if we may contrast with their arbitrary subjective origin, the true conception of History – can attain historical confirmation. The only consistent and worthy method which philosophical investigation can adopt is to take up History where Rationality begins to manifest itself in the actual conduct of the World's affairs (not where it is merely an undeveloped potentiality) – where a condition of things is present in which it realizes itself in consciousness, will and action. The inorganic existence of Spirit – that of abstract Freedom – unconscious *torpidity* in respect to good and evil (and consequently to laws), or, if we please to term it so, "blessed ignorance" – is itself not a subject of History. *Natural,* and at the same time *religious* morality, is the piety of the *family.* In this social relation, morality consists in the members behaving towards each other *not as individuals* – possessing an independent will; not as persons. The Family therefore, is excluded from that process of development in which History takes its rise. But when this self-involved spiritual Unity steps beyond this circle of feeling and natural love, and first attains the consciousness of personality, we have that dark, dull centre of indifference, in which neither Nature nor Spirit is open and transparent; and for which Nature and Spirit can become open and transparent only by means of a further process – a very lengthened culture of that Will at length become self-conscious. Consciousness alone is clearness; and is that alone for which God (or any other existence) can be revealed. In its true form – in absolute universality – nothing can be manifested except to consciousness made percipient of it. Freedom is nothing but the recognition and adoption of such universal substantial objects as Right

71

and Law, and the production of a reality that is accordant with them – the State. Nations may have passed a long life before arriving at this their destination, and during this period, they may have attained considerable culture in some directions. This ante-historical period – consistently with what has been said – lies out of our plan; whether a real history followed it, or the peoples in question never attained a political constitution. – It is a great discovery in history – as of a new world – which has been made within rather more than the last twenty years, respecting the Sanscrit and the connection of the European languages with it. In particular, the connection of the German and Indian peoples has been demonstrated, with as much certainty as such subjects allow of. Even at the present time we know of peoples which scarcely form a society, much less a State, but that have been long known as existing; while with regard to others, which in their advanced condition excite our especial interest, tradition reaches beyond the record of the founding of the State, and they experienced many changes prior to that epoch. In the connection just referred to, between the languages of nations so widely separated, we have a result before us, which proves the diffusion of those nations from Asia as a centre, and the so dissimilar development of what had been originally related, as an incontestable fact; not as an inference deduced by that favorite method of combining, and reasoning from, circumstances grave and trivial, which has already enriched and will continue to enrich history with so many fictions given out as facts. But that apparently so extensive range of events lies beyond the pale of history; in fact preceded it.

In our language the term *History*[5] unites the objective with the subjective side, and denotes quite as much the *historia rerum gestarum,* as the *res gestae* themselves; on the other hand it comprehends not less what has *happened,* than the *narration* of what has happened. This union of the two meanings we must regard as of a higher order than mere outward accident; we must suppose historical narrations to have appeared contemporaneously with historical deeds and events. It is an internal vital principle common to both that produces them synchronously. Family memorials, patriarchal traditions, have an interest confined to the family and the clan. The uniform course of events which such a condition implies, is no subject of serious remembrance; though distinct transactions or turns of fortune, may rouse Mnemosyne to form conceptions of them – in the same way as love and the religious emotions provoke imagination to give shape to a previously formless impulse. But it is the State which first presents subject- matter that is not only *adapted* to the prose of History, but involves the production of such history in the very progress of its own being. Instead of merely subjective mandates on the part of government – sufficing for the needs of the moment – a community that is acquiring a stable existence, and exalting itself into a State, requires formal commands and laws – comprehensive and universally binding prescriptions; and thus produces a record as well as an interest concerned with intelligent, definite – and, in their results – lasting transactions and occurrences; on which Mnemosyne, for the behoof of the perennial object of the formation and constitution of the State, is impelled to confer perpetuity. Profound sentiments generally, such as that of love, as also religious intuition and its conceptions, are in themselves complete – constantly present and satisfying; but that outward existence of a political constitution which is enshrined in its rational laws and customs, is an *imperfect* Present; and cannot be thoroughly understood without a knowledge of the past. The periods – whether we suppose them to be centuries or millennia – that were passed by nations before history was written among them – and which may have been filled with revolutions, nomadic wanderings, and the strangest mutations – are on that very account destitute of *objective* history, because they present no *subjective* history, no annals. We need not suppose that the records of such periods have accidentally perished; rather, because they were not possible, do we find them wanting. Only in a State cognizant of Laws, can distinct transactions take place, accompanied by such a clear consciousness of them as supplies the ability and suggests the necessity of an enduring record. It strikes every one, in beginning to form an acquaintance with the treasures of Indian literature, that a land so rich in intellectual products, and those of the profoundest order of thought, has no History; and in this respect contrasts most strongly with China – an empire possessing one so remarkable, one going back to the most ancient times. India has not only ancient books relating to religion, and splendid poetical productions, but also ancient codes; the existence of which latter kind of literature has been mentioned as a condition necessary to the origination of History –

and yet History itself is not found. But in that country the impulse of organization, in beginning to develop social distinctions, was immediately petrified in the merely natural classification according to *castes*; so that although the laws concern themselves with civil rights, they make even these dependent on natural distinctions; and are especially occupied with determining the relations (Wrongs rather than Rights) of those classes towards each other, *i.e.*, the privileges of the higher over the lower. Consequently, the element of morality is banished from the pomp of Indian life and from its political institutions. Where that iron bondage of distinctions derived from nature prevails, the connection of society is nothing but wild arbitrariness – transient activity – or rather the play of violent emotion without any goal of advancement or development. Therefore no intelligent reminiscence, no object for Mnemosyne presents itself; and imagination – confused though profound – expatiates in a region, which, to be capable of History, must have had an aim within the domain of Reality, and, at the same time, of substantial Freedom.

Since such are the conditions indispensable to a history, it has happened that the growth of Families to Clans, of Clans to Peoples, and their local diffusion consequent upon this numerical increase – a series of facts which itself suggests so many instances of social complication, war, revolution, and ruin – a process which is so rich in interest, and so comprehensive in extent – has occurred without giving rise to History; moreover, that the extension and organic growth of the empire of articulate sounds has itself remained voiceless and dumb – a stealthy, unnoticed advance. It is a fact revealed by philological monuments, that languages, during a rude condition of the nations that have spoken them, have been very highly developed; that the human understanding occupied this theoretical region with great ingenuity and completeness. For Grammar, in its extended and consistent form, is the work of thought, which makes its categories distinctly visible therein. It is, moreover, a fact, that with advancing social and political civilization, this systematic completeness of intelligence suffers attrition, and language thereupon becomes poorer and ruder: a singular phenomenon – that the progress towards a more highly intellectual condition, while expanding and cultivating rationality, should disregard that intelligent amplitude and expressiveness – should find it an obstruction and contrive to do without it. Speech is the act of theoretic intelligence in a special sense; it is its *external* manifestation. Exercises of memory and imagination without language, are direct, [non-speculative] manifestations. But this act of theoretic intelligence itself, as also its subsequent development, and the more concrete class of facts connected with it – viz. the spreading of peoples over the earth, their separation from each other, their comminglings and wanderings – remain involved in the obscurity of a voiceless past. They are not acts of Will becoming self-conscious – of Freedom, mirroring itself in a phenomenal form, and creating for itself a proper reality. Not partaking of this element of substantial, veritable existence, those nations – notwithstanding the development of language among them – never advanced to the possession of a *history*. The rapid growth of language, and the progress and dispersion of Nations, assume importance and interest for concrete Reason, only when they have come in contact with States, or begin to form political constitutions themselves.

After these remarks, relating to the form of the *commencement* of the World's History, and to that ante-historical period which must be excluded from it, we have to state the direction of its course: though here only formally. The further definition of the subject in the concrete comes under the head of arrangement. Universal history – as already demonstrated – shows the development of the consciousness of Freedom on the part of Spirit, and of the consequent realization of that Freedom. This development implies a gradation – a series of increasingly adequate expressions or manifestations of Freedom, which result from its Idea. The logical, and – as still more prominent – the *dialectical* nature of the Idea in general, viz. that it is self-determined – that it assumes successive forms which it successively transcends; and by this very process of transcending its earlier stages gains an affirmative, and, in fact, a richer and more concrete shape; – this necessity of its nature, and the necessary series of pure abstract forms which the Idea successively assumes – is exhibited in the department of *Logic*. Here we need adopt only one of its results, viz. that every step in the process, as differing from any other, has its determinate peculiar principle. In history this principle is idiosyncrasy of Spirit – peculiar National Genius. It is within the

75

limitations of this idiosyncrasy that the spirit of the nation, concretely manifested, expresses every aspect of its consciousness and will – the whole cycle of its realization. Its religion, its polity, its ethics, its legislation, and even its science, art, and mechanical skill, all bear its stamp. These special peculiarities find their key in that common peculiarity – the particular principle that characterizes a people; as, on the other hand, in the facts which History presents in detail, that common characteristic principle may be detected. That such or such a specific quality constitutes the peculiar genius of a people, is the element of our inquiry which must be derived from experience, and historically proved. To accomplish this, presupposes not only a disciplined faculty of abstraction, but an intimate acquaintance with the Idea. The investigator must be familiar *a priori* (if we like to call it so), with the whole circle of conceptions to which the principles in question belong – just as Kepler (to name the most illustrious example in this mode of philosophizing) must have been familiar *a priori* with ellipses, with cubes and squares, and with ideas of their relations, before he could discover, from the empirical data, those immortal "Laws" of his, which are none other than forms of thought pertaining to those classes of conceptions. He who is unfamiliar with the science that embraces these abstract elementary conceptions, is as little capable – though he may have gazed on the firmament and the motions of the celestial bodies for a lifetime – of *understanding* those Laws, as of *discovering* them. From this want of acquaintance with the ideas that relate to the development of Freedom, proceed a part of those objections which are brought against the philosophical consideration of a science usually regarded as one of mere experience; the so- called *a priori* method, and the attempt to insinuate ideas into the empirical data of history, being the chief points in the indictment. Where this deficiency exists, such conceptions appear alien – not lying within the object of investigation. To minds whose training has been narrow and merely subjective – which have not an acquaintance and familiarity with ideas – they are something strange – not embraced in the notion and conception of the subject which their limited intellect forms. Hence the statement that Philosophy does not understand such sciences. It must, indeed, allow that it has not that kind of Understanding which is the prevailing one in the domain of those sciences, that it does not proceed according to the categories of such Understanding, but

76

according to the categories of *Reason* – though at the same time recognizing that Understanding, and its true value and position. It must be observed that in this very process of scientific *Understanding,* it is of importance that the essential should be distinguished and brought into relief in contrast with the so-called non-essential. But in order to render this possible, we must know what *is essential,* and that is – in view of the History of the World in general – the Consciousness of Freedom, and the phases which this consciousness assumes in developing itself. The bearing of historical facts on this category, is their bearing on the truly Essential. Of the difficulties stated, and the opposition exhibited to comprehensive conceptions in science, part must be referred to the inability to grasp and understand Ideas. If in Natural History some monstrous hybrid growth is alleged as an objection to the recognition of clear and indubitable classes or species, a sufficient reply is furnished by a sentiment often vaguely urged – that "the exception confirms the rule"; *i.e.,* that is the part of a well-defined rule, to show the conditions in which it applies, or the deficiency or hybridism of cases that are abnormal. Mere Nature is too weak to keep its genera and species pure, when conflicting with alien elementary influences. If, *e.g.,* on considering the human organization in its concrete aspect, we assert that brain, heart, and so forth are essential to its organic life, some miserable abortion may be adduced, which has on the whole the human form, or parts of it – which has been conceived in a human body and has breathed after birth therefrom – in which nevertheless no brain and no heart is found. If such an instance is quoted against the general conception of a human being – the objector persisting in using the name, coupled with a superficial idea respecting it – it can be proved that a real, concrete human being is a truly different object; that such a being must have a brain in its head, and a heart in its breast.

A similar process of reasoning is adopted, in reference to the correct assertion that genius, talent, moral virtues, and sentiments, and piety, may be found in every zone, under all political constitutions and conditions; in confirmation of which examples are forthcoming in abundance. If, in this assertion, the accompanying distinctions are intended to be repudiated as unimportant or non-essential, reflection evidently limits itself to abstract categories; and ignores the specialities of the object in question, which certainly fall under no principle recognized by such categories. That intellectual position which adopts such merely formal points of view, presents a vast field for ingenious questions, erudite views, and striking comparisons; for profound seeming reflections and declamations, which may be rendered so much the more brilliant in proportion as the subject they refer to is indefinite, and are susceptible of new and varied forms in inverse proportion to the importance of the results that can be gained from them, and the certainty and rationality of their issues. Under such an aspect the well-known Indian Epopees may be compared with the Homeric; perhaps – since it is the vastness of the imagination by which poetical genius proves itself – preferred to them; as, on account of the similarity of single strokes of imagination in the attributes of the divinities, it has been contended that Greek mythological forms may be recognized in those of India. Similarly the Chinese philosophy, as adopting the One [Tov] as its basis, has been alleged to be the same as at a later period appeared as Eleatic philosophy and as the Spinozistic System; while in virtue of its expressing itself also in abstract numbers and lines, Pythagorean and Christian principles have been supposed to be detected in it. Instances of bravery and indomitable courage – traits of magnanimity, of self-denial, and self-sacrifice, which are found among the most savage and the most pusillanimous nations – are regarded as sufficient to support the view that in these nations as much of social virtue and morality may be found as in the most civilized Christian states, or even more. And on this ground a doubt has been suggested whether in the progress of history and of general culture mankind have become better; whether their morality has been increased – morality being regarded in a subjective aspect and view, as founded on what the agent holds to be right and wrong, good and evil; not on a principle which is considered to be in and for itself right and good, or a crime and evil, or on a particular religion believed to be the true one.

We may fairly decline on this occasion the task of tracing the formalism and error of such a view, and establishing the true principles of morality, or rather of social virtue in opposition to false morality. For the History of the World occupies a higher ground than that on which morality has properly its position; which is personal character – the conscience of individuals – their particular will and mode of action; *these* have a value, imputation, reward or punishment proper to themselves. What the absolute aim of Spirit requires and accomplishes – what Providence does – transcends the obligations, and the liability to imputation and the ascription of good or bad motives, which attach to individuality in virtue of its social relations. They who on moral grounds, and consequently with noble intention, have resisted that which the advance of the Spiritual Idea makes necessary, stand higher in moral worth than those whose crimes have been turned into the means – under the direction of a superior principle – of realizing the purposes of that principle. But in such revolutions both parties generally stand within the limits of the same circle of transient and corruptible existence. Consequently it is only a formal rectitude – deserted by the living Spirit and by God – which those who stand upon ancient right and order maintain. The deeds of great men, who are the Individuals of the World's History, thus appear not only justified in view of that intrinsic result of which they were not conscious, but also from the point of view occupied by the secular moralist. But looked at from this point, moral claims that are irrelevant, must not be brought into collision with world- historical deeds and their accomplishment. The Litany of private virtues – modesty, humility, philanthropy and forbearance – must not be raised against them. The History of the World might, on principle, entirely ignore the circle within which morality and the so much talked of distinction between the moral and the politic lies – not only in abstaining from judgments, for the principles involved, and the necessary reference of the deeds in question to those principles, are a sufficient judgment of them – but in leaving Individuals quite out of view and unmentioned. What it has to record is the activity of the Spirit of Peoples, so that the individual forms which that spirit has assumed in the sphere of outward reality, might be left to the delineation of special histories. The same kind of formalism avails itself in its peculiar manner of the indefiniteness attaching to genius, poetry, and even philosophy; thinks equally that it finds these everywhere. We have here products of reflective thought; and it is familiarity with those general conceptions which single out and name real distinctions without fathoming the true depth of the matter – that we call Culture. It is something merely formal, inasmuch as it aims at nothing more than the analysis of the subject, whatever it be, into its constituent parts, and the comprehension of these in their logical definitions and forms. It is not the free universality of conception necessary for making an abstract principle the object of consciousness. Such a consciousness of Thought itself, and of its forms isolated from *a* particular object, is Philosophy. This has, indeed, the condition of its existence in culture; that condition being the taking up of the object of thought, and at the same time clothing it with the form of universality, in such a way that the material content and the form given by the intellect are held in an inseparable state; – inseparable to such a degree that the object in question – which, by the analysis of one conception into a multitude of conceptions, is enlarged to an incalculable treasure of thought – is regarded as a merely empirical datum in whose formation thought has had no share. But it is quite as much an act of Thought – of the Understanding in particular – to embrace in one simple conception object which of itself comprehends a concrete and large significance (as Earth, Man – Alexander or Caesar) and to designate it by one word – as to *resolve* such a conception – duly to isolate in idea the conceptions which it contains, and to give them particular names. And in reference to the view which gave occasion to what has just been said, thus much will be clear – that as reflection produces what we include under the general terms Genius, Talent, Art, Science – formal culture on every grade of intellectual development, not only can, but must grow, and attain a mature bloom, while the grade in question is developing itself to a State, and on this basis of civilization is advancing to intelligent reflection and to general forms of thought – as in laws, so in regard to all else. In the very association of men in a state, lies the necessity of formal culture – consequently of the rise of the sciences and of a cultivated poetry and art generally. The arts designated "plastic," require besides, even in their technical aspect, the civilized association of men. The poetic art – which has less need of external requirements and means, and which has the element of immediate existence, the voice, as its material – steps forth with great boldness and with matured expression, even under the conditions presented by a people not yet united in a political combination; since, as remarked above, language attains on its own particular ground a high intellectual development, prior to the commencement of civilization.

Philosophy also must make its appearance where political life exists; since that in virtue of which any series of phenomena is reduced within the sphere of culture, as above stated, is the Form strictly proper to Thought; and thus for philosophy, which is nothing other than the consciousness of this form itself – the Thinking of Thinking – the material o£ which its edifice is to be constructed, is already prepared by *general* culture. If in the development of the State itself, periods are necessitated which impel the soul of nobler natures to seek refuge from the Present in ideal regions – in order to find in them that harmony with itself which it can no longer enjoy in the discordant real world, where the reflective intelligence attacks all that is holy and deep, which had been spontaneously inwrought into the religion, laws and manners of nations, and brings them down and attenuates them to abstract godless generalities – Thought will be compelled to become Thinking Reason, with the view of effecting in its own element the restoration of its principles from the ruin to which they had been brought.

We find then, it is true, among all world-historical peoples, poetry, plastic art, science, even philosophy; but not only is there a diversity in style and bearing generally, but still more remarkably in subject-matter; and this is a diversity of the most important kind, affecting the rationality of that subject-matter. It is useless for a pretentious aesthetic criticism to demand that our good pleasure should not be made the rule for the matter – the substantial part of their contents – and to maintain that it is the beautiful form as such, the grandeur of the fancy, and so forth, which fine art aims at, and which must be considered and enjoyed by a liberal taste and cultivated mind. A healthy intellect does not tolerate such abstractions, and cannot assimilate productions of the kind above referred to. Granted that the Indian Epopees might be placed on a level with the Homeric, on account of a number of those qualities of form – grandeur of invention and imaginative power, liveliness of images and emotions, and beauty of diction; yet the infinite difference of matter remains; consequently one of substantial importance and involving the interest of Reason, which is immediately concerned with the consciousness of the Idea of Freedom, and its expression in individuals. There is not only a classical *form,* but a classical order of *subject-matter,* and in a work of art form and subject-matter are so closely united that the former can only be classical to the extent to which the latter is so. With a fantastical, indeterminate material – and *Rule* is the essence of *Reason* – the form becomes measureless and formless, or mean and contracted. In the same way, in that comparison of the various systems of philosophy of which we have already spoken, the only point of importance is overlooked, namely, the character of that Unity which is found alike in the Chinese, the Eleatic, and the Spinozistic philosophy – the distinction between the recognition of that Unity as abstract and as concrete – concrete to the extent of being a unity in and by itself – a unity synonymous with Spirit. But that co-ordination proves that it recognizes only such an abstract unity; so that while it gives judgment respecting philosophy, it is ignorant of that very point which constitutes the interest of philosophy.

But there are also spheres which, amid all the variety that is presented in the substantial content of a particular form of culture, remain the same. The difference above-mentioned in art, science, philosophy, concerns the thinking Reason and Freedom, which is the self-consciousness of the former, and which has the same one root with Thought. As it is not the brute, but only the man that thinks, he only – and only because he is a thinking being – has Freedom. *His* consciousness imports this, that the individual comprehends itself as a *person,* that is, recognizes itself in its single existence as possessing universality – as capable of abstraction from, and of surrendering all speciality; and, therefore, as inherently infinite. Consequently those spheres of intelligence which lie beyond the limits of this consciousness are a common ground among those substantial distinctions. Even morality, which is so intimately connected with the consciousness of freedom, can be very pure while that consciousness is still wanting; as far, that is to say, as it expresses duties and rights only as *objective* commands; or even as far as it remains satisfied with the merely formal elevation of the soul – the surrender of the sensual, and of all sensual motives – in a purely negative, self-denying fashion. The *Chinese* morality – since Europeans have become acquainted with it and with the writings of Confucius – has obtained the greatest praise and proportionate attention from those who are familiar with the Christian morality. There is a similar acknowledgment of the sublimity with which the *Indian* religion and poetry, (a statement that must, however, be limited to the higher kind), but especially the Indian philosophy, expatiate upon and demand the removal and sacrifice of sensuality. Yet both these nations are, it must be confessed, *entirely* wanting in the essential consciousness of the Idea of Freedom. To the Chinese their moral laws are just like natural laws – external, positive commands – claims established by force – compulsory duties or rules of courtesy towards each other. Freedom, through which alone the essential determinations of Reason become moral sentiments, is wanting. Morality is a political affair, and its laws are administered by officers of government and legal tribunals. Their treatises upon it, (which are not law books, but are certainly addressed to the subjective will and individual disposition) read – as do the moral writings of the Stoics – like a string of commands stated as necessary for realizing the goal of happiness; so that it seems to be left free to men, on their part, to adopt such commands – to observe them or not; while the conception of an abstract subject, "a wise man" [*Sapiens*] forms the culminating point among the Chinese, as also among the Stoic moralists. Also in the Indian doctrine of the renunciation of the sensuality of desires and earthly interests, positive moral freedom is not the object and end, but the annihilation of consciousness – spiritual and even physical privation of life.

It is the concrete spirit of a people which we have distinctly to recognize, and since it is Spirit it can only be comprehended spiritually, that is, by thought. It is this alone which takes the lead in all the deeds and tendencies of that people, and which is occupied in realizing itself – in satisfying its ideal and becoming self-conscious – for its great business is self-production. But for spirit, the highest attainment is self-knowledge; an advance not only to the *intuition,* but to the *thought* – the clear conception of itself. This it must and is also destined to accomplish; but the accomplishment is at the same time its dissolution, and the rise of another spirit, another world-historical people, another epoch of Universal History. This transition and connection lead us to the connection of the whole – the idea of the World's History as such – which we have now to consider more closely, and of which we have to give a representation.

History in general is therefore the development of Spirit in *Time,* as Nature is the development of the Idea in *Space.* If then we cast a glance over the World's-History generally, we see a vast picture of changes and transactions; of infinitely manifold forms of peoples, states, individuals, in unresting succession. Everything that can enter into and interest the soul of man – all our sensibility to *goodness, beauty, and greatness* – is called into play. On every hand aims are adopted and pursued, which we recognize, whose accomplishment we desire – we hope and fear for them. In all these occurrences and changes we behold human action and suffering predominant; everywhere something akin to ourselves, and therefore everywhere something that excites our interest for or against. Sometimes it attracts us by beauty, freedom, and rich variety, sometimes by energy such as enables even vice to make itself interesting. Sometimes we see the more comprehensive mass of some general interest advancing with comparative slowness, and subsequently sacrificed to an infinite complication of trifling circumstances, and so dissipated into atoms. Then, again, with a vast expenditure of power a trivial result is produced; while from what appears unimportant a tremendous issue proceeds. On every hand there is the motliest throng of events drawing us within the circle of its interest, and when one combination vanishes another immediately appears in its place.

The general thought – the category which first presents itself in this restless mutation of individuals and peoples, existing for a time and then vanishing – is that of *change* at large. The sight of the ruins of some ancient sovereignty directly leads us to contemplate this thought of change in its negative aspect. What traveller among the ruins of Carthage, of Palmyra, Persepolis, or Rome, has not been stimulated to reflections on the transiency of kingdoms and men, and to sadness at the thought of a vigorous and rich life now departed – a sadness which does not expend itself on personal losses and the uncertainty of one's own undertakings, but is a disinterested sorrow at the decay of a splendid and highly cultured national life! But the next consideration which allies itself with that of change, is, that change while it imports dissolution, involves at the same time the rise of a *new life* – that while death is the issue of life, life is also the issue of death. This is a grand conception; one which the Oriental thinkers attained, and which is perhaps the highest in their metaphysics. In the idea of *Metempsychosis* we find it evolved in its relation to individual existence; but a myth more generally known, is that of the *Phoenix* as a type of the Life of *Nature;* eternally preparing for itself its funeral pile, and consuming itself upon it; but so that from its ashes is produced the new, renovated, fresh life. But this image is only Asiatic; oriental not occidental. Spirit – consuming the envelope of its existence – does not merely pass into another envelope, nor rise rejuvenescent from the ashes of its previous form; it comes forth exalted, glorified, a purer spirit. It certainly makes war upon itself – consumes its own existence; but in this very destruction it works up that existence into a new form, and each successive phase becomes in its turn a material, working on which it exalts itself to a new grade.

If we consider Spirit in this aspect – regarding its changes not merely as rejuvenescent transitions, *i.e.,* returns to the same form, but rather as manipulations of itself, by which it multiplies the material for future endeavors – we see it exerting itself in a variety of modes and directions; developing its powers and gratifying its desires in a variety which is inexhaustible; because every one of its creations, in which it has already found gratification, meets it anew as material, and is a new stimulus to plastic activity. The abstract conception of mere change gives place to the thought of Spirit manifesting, developing, and perfecting its powers in every direction which its manifold nature can follow. What powers it inherently possesses we learn from the variety of products and formations which it originates. In this pleasurable activity, it has to do only with itself. As involved with the conditions of mere nature – internal and external – it will indeed meet in these not only opposition and hindrance, but will often see its endeavors thereby fail; often sink under the complications in which it is entangled either by Nature or by itself. But in such case it perishes in fulfilling its own destiny and proper function, and even thus exhibits the spectacle of self-demonstration as spiritual activity.

The very essence of Spirit is activity; it realizes its potentiality – makes itself its own deed, its own work – and thus it becomes an object to itself; contemplates itself as an objective existence. Thus is it with the Spirit of a people: it is a Spirit having strictly defined characteristics, which erects itself into an objective world, that exists and persists in a particular

85

religious form of worship, customs, constitution, and political laws – in the whole complex of its institutions – in the events and transactions that make up its history. That is its work – that is what this particular Nation *is*. Nations are what their deeds are. Every Englishman will say: We are the men who navigate the ocean, and have the commerce of the world; to whom the East Indies belong and their riches; who have a parliament, juries, etc. – The relation of the individual to that Spirit is that he appropriates to himself this substantial existence; that it becomes his character and capability, enabling him to have a definite place in the world – to be *something*. For he finds the being of the people to which he belongs an already established, firm world – objectively present to him – with which he has to incorporate himself. In this its work, therefore – its world – the Spirit of the people enjoys its existence and finds its satisfaction. – A Nation is moral – virtuous – vigorous – while it is engaged in realizing its grand objects, and defends its work against external violence during the process of giving to its purposes an objective existence. The contradiction between its potential, subjective being – its inner aim and life – and its *actual* being is removed; it has attained full reality, has itself objectively present to it. But this having been attained, the activity displayed by the Spirit of the people in question is no longer needed; it has its desire. The Nation can still accomplish much in war and peace at home and abroad; but the living substantial soul itself may be said to have ceased its activity. The essential, supreme interest has consequently vanished from its life, for interest is present only where there is opposition. The nation lives the same kind of life as the individual when passing from maturity to old age – in the enjoyment of itself – in the satisfaction of being exactly what it desired and was able to attain. Although its imagination might have transcended that limit, it nevertheless abandoned any such aspirations as objects of *actual endeavor,* if the real world was less than favorable to their attainment – and restricted its aim by the conditions thus imposed. This mere *customary life* (the watch wound up and going on of itself) is that which brings on natural death. Custom is activity without opposition, for which there remains only a formal duration; in which the fulness and zest that originally characterized the aim of life are out of the question – a merely external sensuous existence which has ceased to throw itself enthusiastically into its object. Thus perish individuals, thus perish peoples by a natural death; and though the latter may continue in being, it is an existence without intellect or vitality; having no need of its institutions, because the need for them is satisfied – a political nullity and tedium. In order that a truly universal interest may arise, the Spirit of a People must advance to the adoption of some new purpose; but whence can this new purpose originate? It would be a higher, more comprehensive conception of itself – a transcending of its principle – but this very act would involve a principle of a new order, a new National Spirit.

Such a new principle does in fact enter into the Spirit of a people that has arrived at full development and self-realization; it dies not a simply natural death – for it is not a mere single individual, but a spiritual, generic life; in its case natural death appears to imply destruction through its own agency. The reason of this difference from the single natural individual, is that the Spirit of a people exists as a *genus,* and consequently carries within it its own negation, in the very generality which characterizes it. A people can only die a violent death when it has become naturally dead in itself, as, *e.g.,* the German Imperial Cities, the German Imperial Constitution.

It is not of the nature of the all-pervading Spirit to die this merely natural death; it does not simply sink into the senile life of mere custom, but – as being a National Spirit belonging to Universal History – attains to the consciousness of what its work is; it attains to a conception of itself. In fact it is world-historical only in so far as a *universal principle* has lain in its fundamental element – in its grand aim: only so far is the work which such a spirit produces, a moral, political organization. If it be mere desires that impel nations to activity, such deeds pass over without leaving a trace; or their traces are only ruin and destruction. Thus, it was first Chronos – Time – that ruled; the Golden Age, without moral products; and what was produced – the offspring of that Chronos – was devoured by it. It was Jupiter – from whose head Minerva sprang, and to whose circle of divinities belong Apollo and the Muses – that first put a constraint upon Time, and set a bound to its principle of decadence. He is the Political god, who produced a moral work – the State.

In the very element of an achievement the quality of generality, of thought, is contained; without thought it has no objectivity; that is its basis. The highest point in the development of a people is this – to have gained a conception of its life and condition – to have reduced its laws, its ideas of justice and morality to a science; for in this unity [of the objective and subjective] lies the most intimate unity that Spirit can attain to in and with itself. In its work it is employed in rendering itself an object of its own contemplation; but it cannot develop itself objectively in its essential nature, except in *thinking* itself.

At this point, then, Spirit is acquainted with its principles – the general character of its acts. But at the same time, in virtue of its very generality, this work of thought is different in point of form from the actual achievements of the national genius, and from the vital agency by which those achievements have been performed. We have then before us a *real* and an *ideal* existence of the Spirit of the Nation. If we wish to gain the general idea and conception of what the Greeks were, we find it in Sophocles and Aristophanes, in Thucydides and Plato. In these individuals the Greek spirit conceived and thought itself. This is the profounder kind of satisfaction which the Spirit of a people attains; but it is "ideal," and distinct from its "real" activity. At such a time, therefore, we are sure to see a people finding satisfaction in the *idea* of virtue; putting *talk* about virtue partly side by side with actual virtue, but partly in the place of it. On the other hand pure, universal thought, since its nature is universality, is apt to bring the Special and Spontaneous – Belief, Trust, Customary Morality – to reflect upon itself, and its primitive simplicity; to show up the limitation with which it is fettered – partly suggesting reasons for renouncing duties, partly itself *demanding reasons,* and the connection of such requirements with Universal Thought; and not finding that connection, seeking to impeach the authority of duty generally, as destitute of a sound foundation.

At the same time the isolation of individuals from each other and from the Whole makes its appearance; their aggressive selfishness and vanity; their seeking personal advantage and consulting this at the expense of the State at large. That inward principle in transcending its outward manifestations is subjective also in *form* – viz., selfishness and corruption in the unbound passions and egotistic interests of men.

88

Zeus, therefore, who is represented as having put a limit to the devouring agency of Time, and stayed this transiency by having established something inherently and independently durable – Zeus and his race are themselves swallowed up, and that by the very power that produced them – the principle of thought, perception, reasoning, insight derived from rational grounds, and the requirement of such grounds.

Time is the negative element in the sensuous world. Thought is the same negativity, but it is the deepest, the infinite form of it, in which therefore all existence generally is dissolved; first *finite* existence – *determinate,* limited form: but existence *generally,* in its objective character, is limited; it appears therefore as a mere datum – something immediate – authority; – and is either intrinsically finite and limited, or presents itself as a limit for the thinking subject, and its infinite reflection on itself [unlimited abstraction].

But first we must observe how the life which proceeds from death, is itself, on the other hand, only individual life; so that, regarding the species as the real and substantial in this vicissitude, the perishing of the individual is a regress of the species into individuality. The perpetuation of the race is, therefore, none other than the monotonous repetition of the same kind of existence. Further, we must remark how perception – the comprehension of being by thought – is the source and birthplace of a new, and in fact higher form, in a principle which while it preserves, dignifies its material. For Thought is that *Universal* – that *Species* which is immortal, which preserves identity with itself. The particular form of Spirit not merely passes away in the world by natural causes in Time, but is annulled in the automatic self-mirroring activity of consciousness. Because this annulling is an activity of Thought, it is at the same time conservative and elevating in its operation. While then, on the one side, Spirit annuls the reality, the permanence of that which it *is,* it gains on the other side, the essence, the Thought, the Universal element of that which *it only was* [its transient conditions]. Its principle is no longer that immediate import and aim which it was previously, but the *essence* of that import and aim.

The result of this process is then that Spirit, in rendering itself objective and making this its being an object of thought, on the one hand destroys the determinate form of its being, on the other hand gains a comprehension of the universal element which it involves, and thereby gives a new form to its inherent principle. In virtue of this, the substantial character of the National Spirit has been altered – that is, its principle has risen into another, and in fact a higher principle.

It is of the highest importance in apprehending and comprehending History to have and to understand the thought involved in this transition. The individual traverses as a unity various grades of development, and remains the same individual; in like manner also does a people, till the Spirit which it embodies reaches the grade of universality. In this point lies the fundamental, the Ideal necessity of transition. This is the soul – the essential consideration – of the philosophical comprehension of History.

Spirit is essentially the result of its own activity: its activity is the transcending of immediate, simple, unreflected existence – the negation of that existence, and the returning into itself. We may compare it with the seed; for with this the plant begins, yet it is also the result of the plant's entire life. But the weak side of life is exhibited in the fact that the commencement and the result are disjoined from each other. Thus also is it in the life of individuals and peoples. The life of a people ripens a certain fruit; its activity aims at the complete manifestation of the principle which it embodies. But this fruit does not fall back into the bosom of the people that produced and matured it; on the contrary, it becomes a poison-draught to it. That poison-draught it cannot let alone, for it has an insatiable thirst for it: the taste of the draught is its annihilation, though at the same time the rise of a new principle.

We have already discussed the final aim of this progression. The principles of the successive phases of Spirit that animate the Nations in a necessitated gradation, are themselves only steps in the development of the one universal Spirit, which through them elevates and completes itself to a self-comprehending *totality*. While we are thus concerned exclusively with the Idea of Spirit, and in the History of the World regard everything as only its manifestation, we have, in traversing the past – however extensive its periods – only to do with what is *present;* for philosophy, as occupying itself with the True, has to do with the *eternally present.* Nothing in the past is lost for it, for the Idea is ever present; Spirit is immortal; with it there is no past, no future, but an essential *now.* This necessarily implies that the present form of Spirit comprehends within it all earlier steps. These have indeed unfolded themselves in succession independently; but what Spirit is it has always been essentially; distinctions are only the development of this essential nature. The life of the ever present Spirit is a circle of progressive embodiments, which looked at in one aspect still exist beside each other, and only as looked at from another point of view appear as past. The grades which Spirit seems to have left behind it, it still possesses in the depths of its present.

GEOGRAPHICAL BASIS OF HISTORY

Contrasted with the universality of the moral Whole and with the unity of that individuality which is its active principle, the *natural* connection that helps to produce the Spirit of a People, appears an extrinsic element; but inasmuch as we must regard it as the ground on which that Spirit plays its part, it is an *essential* and *necessary* basis. We began with the assertion that, in the History of the World, the Idea of Spirit appears in its actual embodiment as a series of external forms, each one of which declares itself as an actually existing people. This existence falls under the category of Time as well as Space, in the way of natural existence; and the special principle, which every world-historical people embodies, has this principle at the same time as a *natural* characteristic. Spirit, clothing itself in this form of nature, suffers its particular phases to assume separate existence; for mutual exclusion is the mode of existence proper to mere nature. These natural distinctions must be first of all regarded as special possibilities, from which the Spirit of the people in question germinates, and among them is the Geographical Basis. It is not our concern to become acquainted with the land occupied by nations as an external locale, but with the natural type of the locality, as intimately connected with the type and character of the people which is the offspring of such a soil. This character is nothing more nor less than the mode and form in which nations make their appearance in History, and take place and position in it. Nature should not be rated too high nor too low: the mild Ionic sky certainly contributed much to the charm of the Homeric poems, yet this alone can produce no Homers. Nor in fact does it continue to produce them; under Turkish government no bards have arisen. We must first take notice of those natural conditions which have to be excluded once for all from the drama of the World's History. In the Frigid and in the Torrid zone the locality of World-historical peoples cannot be found. For awakening consciousness takes its rise surrounded by natural influences alone, and every development of it is the reflection of Spirit back upon itself in opposition to the immediate, unreflected character of mere nature. Nature is therefore one element in this antithetic abstracting process; Nature is the first standpoint from which man can gain freedom within himself, and this liberation must not be rendered difficult by natural obstructions. Nature, as contrasted with Spirit, is a quantitative mass, whose power must not be so great as to make its single force omnipotent. In the extreme zones man cannot come to free movement; cold and heat are here too powerful to allow Spirit to build up a world for *itself*. Aristotle said long ago, "When pressing needs are satisfied, man turns to the general and more elevated." But in the extreme zones such pressure may be said never to cease, never to be warded off; men are constantly impelled to direct attention to nature, to the glowing rays of the sun, and the icy frost. The true theatre of History is therefore the temperate zone; or, rather, its northern half, because the earth there presents itself in a continental form, and has a broad breast, as the Greeks say. In the south, on the contrary, it divides itself, and runs out into many points. The same peculiarity shows itself in natural products. The north has many kinds of animals and plants with common characteristics; in the south, where the land divides itself into points, natural forms also present individual features contrasted with each other.

The World is divided into *Old* and *New;* the name of *New* having originated in the fact that America and Australia have only lately become known to us. But these parts of the world are not only relatively new, but intrinsically so in respect of their entire physical and psychical constitution. Their geological antiquity we have nothing to do with. I will not deny the New World the honor of having emerged from the sea at the world's formation contemporaneously with the old: yet the Archipelago between South America and Asia shows a physical immaturity. The greater part of the islands are so constituted, that they are, as it were, only a superficial deposit of earth over rocks, which shoot up from the fathomless deep, and bear the character of novel origination. New Holland shows a not less immature geographical character; for in penetrating from the settlements of the English farther into the country, we discover immense streams, which have not yet developed themselves to such a degree as to dig a channel for themselves, but lose themselves in marshes. Of America and its grade of civilization, especially in Mexico and Peru, we have information, but it imports nothing more than that this culture was an entirely national one, which must expire as soon as Spirit approached it. America has always shown itself physically and psychically powerless, and still shows itself so. For the aborigines, after the landing of the Europeans in America, gradually vanished at the breath of European activity. In the United States of North America all the citizens are of European descent, with whom the old inhabitants could not amalgamate, but were driven back. The aborigines have certainly adopted some arts and usages from the Europeans, among others that of brandy-drinking, which has operated with deadly effect. In the South the natives were treated with much greater violence, and employed in hard labors to which their strength was by no means competent. A mild and passionless disposition, want of spirit, and a crouching submissiveness towards a Creole, and still more towards a European, are the chief characteristics of the native Americans; and it will be long before the Europeans succeed in producing any independence of feeling in them. The inferiority of these individuals in all respects, even in regard to size, is very manifest; only the quite southern races in Patagonia are more vigorous natures, but still abiding in their natural condition of rudeness and barbarism. When the Jesuits and the Catholic clergy proposed to accustom the Indians to European culture and manners (they have, as is well known, founded a state in Paraguay and convents in Mexico and California), they commenced a close intimacy with them, and prescribed for them the duties of the day, which, slothful though their disposition was, they complied with under the authority of the Friars. These prescripts (at midnight a bell had to remind them even of their matrimonial duties), were first, and very wisely, directed to the creation of wants – the springs of human activity generally. The weakness of the American physique was a chief reason for bringing the negroes to America, to employ their labor in the work that had to be done in the New World; for the negroes are far more susceptible of European culture than the Indians, and an English traveller has adduced instances of negroes having become competent clergymen, medical men, etc. (a negro first discovered the use of the Peruvian bark), while only a single native was known to him whose

94

intellect was sufficiently developed to enable him to study, but who had died soon after beginning, through excessive brandy-drinking. The weakness of the human physique of America has been aggravated by a deficiency in the mere tools and appliances of progress – the want of *horses* and *iron*, the chief instruments by which they were subdued.

The original nation having vanished or nearly so, the effective population comes for the most part from Europe; and what takes place in America, is but an emanation from Europe. Europe has sent its surplus population to America in much the same way as from the old Imperial Cities, where trade-guilds were dominant and trade was stereotyped, many persons escaped to other towns which were not under such a yoke, and where the burden of imposts was not so heavy. Thus arose, by the side of Hamburg, Altona – by Frankfort, Offenbach – by Nürnburg, Fürth – and Carouge by Geneva. The relation between North America and Europe is similar. Many Englishmen have settled there, where burdens and imposts do not exist, and where the combination of European appliances and European ingenuity has availed to realize some produce from the extensive and still virgin soil. Indeed the emigration in question offers many advantages. The emigrants have got rid of much that might be obstructive to their interests at home, while they take with them the advantages of European independence of spirit, and acquired skill; while for those who are willing to work vigorously, but who have not found in Europe opportunities for doing so, a sphere of action is certainly presented in America.

America, as is well known, is divided into two parts, connected indeed by an isthmus, but which has not been the means of establishing intercourse between them. Rather, these two divisions are most decidedly distinct from each other. North America shows us on approaching it, along its eastern shore a wide border of level coast, behind which is stretched a chain of mountains – the blue mountains or Appalachians; further north the Alleghanies. Streams issuing from them water the country towards the coast, which affords advantages of the most desirable kind to the United States, whose origin belongs to this region. Behind that mountain-chain the St. Lawrence river flows (in connection with huge lakes), from south to north, and on this river lie the northern colonies of Canada. Farther west we meet the basin of the vast Mississippi, and the basins of the Missouri and Ohio, which it receives, and then debouches into the Gulf of Mexico. On the western side of this region we have in like manner a long mountain chain, running through Mexico and the Isthmus of Panama, and under the names of the Andes or Cordillera, cutting off an edge of coast along the whole west side of South America. The border formed by this is narrower and offers fewer advantages than that of North America. There lie Peru and Chili. On the east side flow eastward the monstrous streams of the Orinoco and Amazons; they form great valleys, not adapted however for cultivation, since they are only wide desert steppes. Towards the south flows the Rio de la Plata, whose tributaries have their origin partly in the Cordilleras, partly in the northern chain of mountains which separates the basin of the Amazon from its own. To the district of the Rio de la Plata belong Brazil, and the Spanish Republics. Colombia is the northern coast-land of South America, at the west of which, flowing along the Andes, the Magdalena debouches into the Caribbean Sea.

With the exception of Brazil, republics have come to occupy South as well as North America. In comparing South America (reckoning Mexico as part of it) with North America, we observe an astonishing contrast.

In North America we witness a prosperous state of things; an increase of industry and population civil order and firm freedom; the whole federation constitutes but a single state, and has its political centres. In South America, on the contrary, the republics depend only on military force; their whole history is a continued revolution; federated states become disunited; others previously separated become united; and all these changes originate in military revolutions. The more special differences between the two parts of America show us two opposite directions, the one in political respects, the other in regard to religion. South America, where the Spaniards settled and asserted supremacy, is Catholic; North America, although a land of sects of every name, is yet fundamentally, Protestant. A wider distinction is presented in the fact, that South America was conquered, but North America colonized. The Spaniards took possession of South America to govern it, and to become rich through occupying political offices, and by exactions. Depending on a very distant mother country, their desires found a larger scope, and by force, address and confidence they gained a great predominance over the

Indians. The North American States were, on the other hand, entirely *colonised,* by Europeans, Since in England Puritans, Episcopalians, and Catholics were engaged in perpetual conflict, and now one party, now the other, had the upper hand, many emigrated to seek religious freedom on a foreign shore. These were industrious Europeans, who betook themselves to agriculture, tobacco and cotton planting, etc. Soon the whole attention of the inhabitants was given to labor, and the basis of their existence as a united body lay in the necessities that bind man to man, the desire of repose, the establishment of civil rights, security and freedom, and a community arising from the aggregation of individuals as atomic constituents; so that the state was merely something external for the protection of property. From the Protestant religion sprang the principle of the mutual confidence of individuals – trust in the honorable dispositions of other men; for in the Protestant Church the entire life – its activity generally – is the field for what it deems religious works. Among Catholics, on the contrary, the basis of such a confidence cannot exist; for in secular matters only force and voluntary subservience are the principles of action; and the forms which are called Constitutions are in this case only a resort of necessity, and are no protection against mistrust. If we compare North America further with Europe, we shall find in the former the permanent example of a republican constitution. A subjective unity presents itself; for there is a President at the head of the State, who, for the sake of security against any monarchical ambition, is chosen only for four years. Universal protection for property, and a something approaching entire immunity from public burdens, are facts which are constantly held up to commendation. We have in these facts the fundamental character of the community – the endeavor of the individual after acquisition, commercial profit, and gain; the preponderance of *private* interest, devoting itself to that of the community only for its own advantage. We find, certainly, legal relations – a formal code of laws; but respect for law exists apart from genuine probity, and the American merchants commonly lie under the imputation of dishonest dealings under legal protection. If, on the one side, the Protestant Church develops the essential principle of confidence, as already stated, it thereby involves on the other hand the recognition of the validity of the element of feeling to such a degree as gives encouragement to unseemly varieties of caprice. Those who adopt this standpoint maintain, that, as everyone may have his peculiar way of viewing things *generally,* so he may have also a *religion* peculiar to himself. Thence the splitting up into so many sects, which reach the very acme of absurdity; many of which have a form of worship consisting in convulsive movements, and sometimes in the most sensuous extravagances. This complete freedom of worship is developed to such a degree, that the various congregations choose ministers and dismiss them according to their absolute pleasure; for the Church is no independent existence – having a substantial spiritual being, and correspondingly permanent external arrangement – but the affairs of religion are regulated by the good pleasure for the time being of the members of the community. In North America the most unbounded license of imagination in religious matters prevails, and that religious unity is wanting which has been maintained in European States, where deviations are limited to a few confessions. As to the political condition of North America, the general object of the existence of this State is not yet fixed and determined, and the necessity for a firm combination does not yet exist; for a real State and a real Government arise only after a distinction of classes has arisen, when wealth and poverty become extreme, and when such a condition of things presents itself that a large portion of the people can no longer satisfy its necessities in the way in which it has been accustomed so to do. But America is hitherto exempt from this pressure, for it has the outlet of colonization constantly and widely open, and multitudes are continually streaming into the plains of the Mississippi. By this means the chief source of discontent is removed, and the continuation of the existing civil condition is guaranteed. A comparison of the United States of North America with European lands is therefore impossible; for in Europe, such a natural outlet for population, notwithstanding all the emigrations that take place, does not exist. Had the woods of Germany been in existence, the French Revolution would not have occurred. North America will be comparable with Europe only after the immeasurable space which that country presents to its inhabitants shall have been occupied, and the members of the political body shall have begun to be pressed back on each other. North America is still in the condition of having land to begin to cultivate. Only when, as in Europe, the direct increase of agriculturists is checked, will the inhabitants, instead of pressing outwards to occupy the fields, press inwards upon each other – pursuing town occupations, and trading with their fellow-citizens; and so form a compact system of civil society, and require an organized state. The North American Federation have no neighboring State (towards which they occupy a relation similar to that of European States to each other), one which they regard with mistrust, and against which they must keep up a standing army. Canada and Mexico are not objects of fear, and England has had fifty years' experience, that *free* America is more profitable to her than it was in a state of *dependence.* The militia of the North American Republic proved themselves quite as brave in the War of Independence as the Dutch under Philip II; but generally, where Independence is not at stake, less power is displayed, and in the year 1814 the militia held out but indifferently against the English.

America is therefore the land of the future, where, in the ages that lie before us, the burden of the World's History shall reveal itself – perhaps in a contest between North and South America. It is a land of desire for all those who are weary of the historical lumber-room of old Europe. Napoleon is reported to have said: "*Cette vieille Europe m'ennuie.*" It is for America to abandon the ground on which hitherto the History of the World has developed itself. What *has* taken place in the New World up to the present time is only an echo of the Old World – the expression of a foreign Life; and as a Land of the Future, it has no interest for us here, for, as regards *History,* our concern must be with that which has been and that which is. In regard to *Philosophy,* on the other hand, we have to do with that which (strictly speaking) is neither past nor future, but with that which *is,* which has an eternal existence – with Reason; and this is quite sufficient to occupy us.

Dismissing, then, the New World, and the dreams to which it may give rise, we pass over to the Old World – the scene of the World's History; and must first direct attention to the natural elements and conditions of existence which it presents. America is divided into two parts, which are indeed connected by an Isthmus, but which forms only an external, material bond of union. The Old World, on the contrary, which lies opposite to America, and is separated from it by the Atlantic Ocean, has its continuity interrupted by a deep inlet – the Mediterranean Sea. The three Continents that compose it have an essential relation to each other, and constitute a totality. Their peculiar feature is that they lie round this Sea, and therefore have an easy means of communication; for rivers and seas are not to be regarded as disjoining, but as uniting. England and Brittany, Norway and Denmark, Sweden and Livonia, have been united. For the three quarters of the globe the Mediterranean Sea is similarly the uniting element, and the centre of World-History. Greece lies here, the focus of light in History. Then in Syria we have Jerusalem, the centre of Judaism and of Christianity; southeast of it lie Mecca and Medina, the cradle of the Mussulman faith; towards the west Delphi and Athens; farther west still, Rome: on the Mediterranean Sea we have also Alexandria and Carthage. The Mediterranean is thus the heart of the Old World, for it is that which conditioned and vitalized it. Without it the History of the World could not be conceived: it would be like ancient Rome or Athens without the forum, where all the life of the city came together. The extensive tract of eastern Asia is severed from the process of general historical development, and has no share in it; so also Northern Europe, which took part in the World's History only at a later date, and had no part in it while the Old World lasted; for this was exclusively limited to the countries lying round the Mediterranean Sea. Julius Caesar's crossing the Alps – the conquest of Gaul and the relation into which the Germans thereby entered with the Roman Empire – makes consequently an epoch in History; for in virtue of this it begins to extend its boundaries beyond the Alps. Eastern Asia and that trans-Alpine country are the extremes of this agitated focus of human life around the Mediterranean – the beginning and end of History – its rise and decline.

The more special geographical distinctions must now be established, and they are to be regarded as essential, rational distinctions, in contrast with the variety of merely accidental circumstances. Of these characteristic differences there are three:

(1) The arid elevated land with its extensive steppes and plains.

(2) The valley plains – the Land of Transition permeated and watered by great Streams.

(3) The coast region in immediate connection with the sea.

These three geographical elements are the essential ones, and we shall see each quarter of the globe triply divided accordingly. The first is the substantial, unvarying, metallic, elevated region, intractably shut up within itself, but perhaps adapted to send forth impulses over the rest of the world; the second forms centres of civilization, and is the yet undeveloped independence [of humanity]; the third offers the means of connecting the world together, and of maintaining the connection.

(1) *The elevated land.* – We see such a description of country in middle Asia inhabited by Mongolians (using the word in a general sense): from the Caspian Sea these Steppes stretch in a northerly direction towards the Black Sea. As similar tracts may be cited the deserts of Arabia and of Barbary in Africa; in South America the country round the Orinoco, and in Paraguay. The peculiarity of the inhabitants of this elevated region, which is watered sometimes only by rain, or by the overflowing of a river (as are the plains of the Orinoco) – is the patriarchal life, the division into single families. The region which these families occupy is unfruitful or productive

Only temporarily: the inhabitants have their property not in the land – from which they derive only a trifling profit – but in the animals that wander with them. For a long time these find pasture in the plains, and when they are depastured, the tribe moves to other parts of the country. They are careless and provide nothing for the winter, on which account therefore, half of the herd is frequently cut off. Among these inhabitants of the upland there exist no legal relations, and consequently there are exhibited among them the extremes of hospitality and rapine; the last more especially when they are surrounded by civilized nations, as the Arabians, who are assisted in their depredations by their horses and camels. The Mongolians feed on mares' milk, and thus the horse supplies them at the same time with appliances for nourishment and for war. Although this is the form of their patriarchal life, it often happens that they cohere together in great masses, and by an impulse of one kind or another, are excited to external movement. Though previously of peaceful disposition, they then rush as a devastating inundation over civilized lands, and the revolution which ensues has no other result than destruction and desolation. Such an agitation was excited among those tribes under Genghis Khan and Tamerlane: they destroyed all before

101

them; then vanished again, as does an overwhelming Forest-torrent – possessing no inherent principle of vitality. From the uplands they rush down into the dells: there dwell peaceful mountaineers – herdsmen who also occupy themselves with agriculture, as do the Swiss. Asia has also such a people: they are however on the whole a less important element.

(2) *The valley plains.* – These are plains, permeated by rivers, and which owe the whole of their fertility to the streams by which they are formed. Such a Valley-Plain is China – India, traversed by the Indus and the Ganges – Babylonia, where the Euphrates and the Tigris flow – Egypt, watered by the Nile. In these regions extensive Kingdoms arise, and the foundation of great States begins. For agriculture, which prevails here as the primary principle of subsistence for individuals, is assisted by the regularity of seasons, which require corresponding agricultural operations; property in land commences, and the consequent legal relations; – that is to say, the basis and foundation of the State, which becomes possible only in connection with such relations.

(3) *The coast land.* – A River divides districts of country from each other, but still more does the sea; and we are accustomed to regard water as the separating element. Especially in recent times has it been insisted upon that States must necessarily have been separated by natural features. Yet on the contrary, it may be asserted as a fundamental principle that nothing *unites* so much as water, for countries are nothing else than districts occupied by streams. Silesia, for instance, is the valley of the Oder; Bohemia and Saxony are the valley of the Elbe; Egypt is the valley of the Nile. With the sea this is not less the case, as has been already pointed out. Only Mountains separate. Thus the Pyrenees decidedly separate Spain from France. The Europeans have been in constant connection with America and the East Indies ever since they were discovered; but they have scarcely penetrated into the interior of Africa and Asia, because intercourse by land is much more difficult than by water. Only through the fact of being a sea, has the Mediterranean become a focus of national life. Let us now look at the character of the nations that are conditioned by this third element.

The sea gives us the idea of the indefinite, the unlimited, and infinite; and in *feeling his own infinite* in that Infinite, man is stimulated and emboldened to stretch beyond the limited: the sea invites man to conquest, and to piratical plunder, but also to honest gain and to commerce. The land, the mere Valley-plain attaches him to the soil; it involves him in an infinite multitude of dependencies, but the sea carries him out beyond these limited circles of thought and action. Those who navigate the sea, have indeed gain for their object, but the means are in this respect paradoxical, inasmuch as they hazard both property and life to attain it. The means therefore are the very opposite to that which they aim at. This is what exalts their gain and occupation above itself, and makes it something brave and noble. Courage is necessarily introduced into trade, daring is joined with wisdom. For the daring which encounters the sea must at the same time embrace wariness – cunning – since it has to do with the treacherous, the most unreliable and deceitful element. This boundless plain is absolutely yielding – withstanding no pressure, not even a breath of wind. It looks boundlessly innocent, submissive, friendly, and insinuating; and it is exactly this submissiveness which changes the sea into the most dangerous and violent element. To this deceitfulness and violence man opposes merely a simple piece of wood; confides entirely in his courage and presence of mind; and thus passes from a firm ground to an unstable support, taking his artificial ground with him. The Ship – that swan of the sea, which cuts the watery plain in agile and arching movements or describes circles upon it – is a machine whose invention does the greatest honor to the boldness of man as well as to his understanding. This stretching out of the sea beyond the limitations of the land, is wanting to the splendid political edifices of Asiatic States, although they themselves border on the sea – as for example, China. For them the sea is only the limit, the ceasing of the land; they have no positive relation to it. The activity to which the sea invites, is a quite peculiar one: thence arises the fact that the coast-lands almost always separate themselves from the states of the interior although they are connected with these by a river. Thus Holland has severed itself from Germany, Portugal from Spain.

In accordance with these data we may now consider the three portions of the globe with which History is concerned, and here the three characteristic principles manifest themselves in a more or less striking manner: Africa has for its leading classical feature the Upland, Asia the contrast of river regions with the Upland, Europe the mingling of these several elements. *Africa* must be divided into three parts: one is that which lies south of the desert of Sahara – Africa proper – the Upland almost entirely unknown to us, with narrow coast-tracts along the sea; the second is that to the north of the desert – European Africa (if we may so call it) – a coastland; the third is the river region of the Nile, the only valley-land of Africa, and which is in connection with Asia.

Africa proper, as far as History goes back, has remained – for all purposes of connection with the rest of the World – shut up; it is the Gold-land compressed within itself – the land of childhood, which lying beyond the day of self-conscious history, is enveloped in the dark mantle of Night. Its isolated character originates, not merely in its tropical nature, but essentially in its geographical condition. The triangle which it forms (if we take the West Coast – which in the Gulf of Guinea makes a strongly indented angle – for one side, and in the same way the East Coast to Cape Gardafu for another) is on two sides so constituted for the most part, as to have a very narrow Coast Tract, habitable only in a few isolated spots. Next to this towards the interior, follows to almost the same extent, a girdle of marsh land with the most luxuriant vegetation, the especial home of ravenous beasts, snakes of all kinds – a border tract whose atmosphere is poisonous to Europeans. This border constitutes the base of a cincture of high mountains, which are only at distant intervals traversed by streams, and where they are so, in such a way as to form no means of union with the interior; for the interruption occurs but seldom below the upper part of the mountain ranges, and only in individual narrow channels, where are frequently found innavigable waterfalls and torrents crossing each other in wild confusion. During the three or three and a half centuries that the Europeans have known this border-land and have taken places in it into their possession, they have only here and there (and that but for a short time) passed these mountains, and have nowhere settled down beyond them. The land surrounded by these mountains is an unknown Upland, from which on the other hand the Negroes have seldom made their way through. In the sixteenth century occurred at many very distant points, outbreaks of terrible hordes which rushed down upon the more peaceful inhabitants of the declivities. Whether any internal movement had taken place, or if so, of what

104

character, we do not know. What we do know of these hordes, is the contrast between their conduct in their wars and forays themselves – which exhibited the most reckless inhumanity and disgusting barbarism – and the fact that afterwards, when their rage was spent, in the calm time of peace, they showed themselves mild and well disposed towards the Europeans, when they became acquainted with them. This holds good of the Fullahs and of the Mandingo tribes, who inhabit the mountain terraces of the Senegal and Gambia. The second portion of Africa is the river district of the Nile – Egypt; which was adapted to become a mighty centre of independent civilization, and therefore is as isolated and singular in Africa as Africa itself appears in relation to the other parts of the world. The northern part of Africa, which may be specially called that of the *coast- territory* (for Egypt has been frequently driven back on itself, by the Mediterranean) lies on the Mediterranean and the Atlantic; a magnificent territory, on which Carthage once lay – the site of the modern Morocco, Algiers, Tunis, and Tripoli. This part was to be – *must* be attached to Europe: the French have lately made a successful effort in this direction: like Hither- Asia, it looks Europe-wards. Here in their turn have Carthaginians, Romans, and Byzantines, Mussulmans, Arabians, had their abode, and the interests of Europe have always striven to get a footing in it.

The peculiarly African character is difficult to comprehend, for the very reason that in reference to it, we must quite give up the principle which naturally accompanies all *our* ideas – the category of Universality. In Negro life the characteristic point is the fact that consciousness has not yet attained to the realization of any substantial objective existence – as for example, God, or Law – in which the interest of man's volition is involved and in which he realizes his own being. This distinction between himself as an individual and the universality of his essential being, the African in the uniform, undeveloped oneness of his existence has not yet attained; so that the Knowledge of an absolute Being, an Other and a Higher than his individual self, is entirely wanting. The Negro, as already observed, exhibits the natural man in his completely wild and untamed state. We must lay aside all thought of reverence and morality – all that we call feeling – if we would rightly comprehend him; there is nothing harmonious with humanity to be found in this type of character. The copious and circumstantial accounts of Missionaries completely confirm this, and Mahommedanism appears to be the only thing which in any way brings the Negroes within the range of culture. The Ma-hommedans too understand better than the Europeans, how to penetrate into the interior of the country. The grade of culture which the Negroes occupy may be more nearly appreciated by considering the aspect which *Religion* presents among them. That which forms the basis of religious conceptions is the consciousness on the part of man of a Higher Power – even though this is conceived only as a *vis natures* – in relation to which he feels himself a weaker, humbler being. Religion begins with the consciousness that there is something higher than man. But even Herodotus called the Negroes sorcerers: – now in *Sorcery* we have not the idea of a God, of a moral faith; it exhibits man as the highest power, regarding him as alone occupying a position of command over the power of Nature. We have here therefore nothing to do with a spiritual adoration of God, nor with an empire of Right. God thunders, but is not on that account recognized as God. For the soul of man, God must be more than a thunderer, whereas among the Negroes this is not the case. Although they are necessarily conscious of dependence upon nature – for they need the beneficial influence of storm, rain, cessation of the rainy period, and so on – yet this does not conduct them to the consciousness of a Higher Power: it is they who command the elements, and this they call "magic." The Kings have a class of ministers through whom they command elemental changes, and every place possesses such magicians, who perform special ceremonies, with all sorts of gesticulations, dances, uproar, and shouting, and in the midst of this confusion commence their incantations. The second element in their religion, consists in their giving an outward form to this supernatural power – projecting their hidden might into the world of phenomena by means of images. What they conceive of as the power in question, is therefore nothing really objective, having a substantial being and different from themselves, but the first thing that comes in their way. This, taken quite indiscriminately, they exalt to the dignity of a "Genius"; it may be an animal, a tree, a stone, or a wooden figure. This is their *Fetich* – a word to which the Portuguese first gave currency, and which is derived from *feitizo,* magic. Here, in the Fetich, a kind of objective independence as contrasted with the arbitrary fancy of the individual

106

seems to manifest itself; but as the objectivity is nothing other than the fancy of the individual projecting itself into space, the human individuality remains master of the image it has adopted. If any mischance occurs which the Fetich has not averted, if rain is suspended, if there is a failure in the crops, they bind and beat or destroy the Fetich and so get rid of it, making another immediately, and thus holding it in their own power. Such a Fetich has no independence as an object of religious worship; still less has it aesthetic independence as a work of art; it is merely a creation that expresses the arbitrary choice of its maker, and which always remains in his hands. In short there is no relation of dependence in this religion. There is however one feature that points to something beyond; – the *Worship of the Dead* – in which their deceased forefathers and ancestors are regarded by them as a power influencing the living. Their idea in the matter is that these ancestors exercise vengeance and inflict upon man various injuries – exactly in the sense in which this was supposed of witches in the Middle Ages. Yet the power of the dead is not held superior to that of the living, for the Negroes command the dead and lay spells upon them. Thus the power in question remains substantially always in bondage to the living subject. Death itself is looked upon by the Negroes as no universal natural law; even this, they think, proceeds from evil-disposed magicians. In this doctrine is certainly involved the elevation of man over Nature; to such a degree that the chance volition of man is superior to the merely natural – that he looks upon this as an instrument to which he does not pay the compliment of treating it in a way conditioned by itself, but which he commands.[6]

But from the fact that man is regarded as the Highest, it follows that he has no respect for himself; for only with the consciousness of a Higher Being does he reach a point of view which inspires him with real reverence. For if arbitrary choice is the absolute, the only substantial objectivity that is realized, the mind cannot in such be conscious of any Universality. The Negroes indulge, therefore, that perfect *contempt* for humanity, which in its bearing on Justice and Morality is the fundamental characteristic of the race. They have moreover no knowledge of the immortality of the soul, although spectres are supposed to appear. The undervaluing of humanity among them reaches an incredible degree of intensity. Tyranny is regarded as no wrong, and cannibalism *is* looked upon as quite customary and proper. Among us instinct deters from it, if we can speak of instinct at all as appertaining to man. But with the Negro this is not the case, and the devouring of human flesh is altogether consonant with the general principles of the African race; to the sensual Negro, human flesh is but an object of sense – mere flesh. At the death of a King hundreds are killed and eaten; prisoners are butchered and their flesh sold in the markets; the victor is accustomed to eat the heart of his slain foe. When magical rites are performed, it frequently happens that the sorcerer kills the first that comes in his way and divides his body among the bystanders. Another characteristic fact in reference to the Negroes is Slavery. Negroes are enslaved by Europeans and sold to America. Bad as this may be, their lot in their own land is even worse, since there a slavery quite as absolute exists; for it is the essential principle of slavery, that man has not yet attained a consciousness of his freedom, and consequently sinks down to a mere Thing – an object of no value. Among the Negroes moral sentiments are quite weak, or more strictly speaking, non-existent. Parents sell their children, and conversely children their parents, as either has the opportunity. Through the pervading influence of slavery all those bonds of moral regard which we cherish towards each other disappear, and it does not occur to the Negro mind to expect from others what we are enabled to claim. The polygamy of the Negroes has frequently for its object the having many children, to be sold, every one of them, into slavery; and very often naive complaints on this score are heard, as for instance in the case of a Negro in London, who lamented that he was now quite a poor man because he had already sold all his relations. In the contempt of humanity displayed by the Negroes, it is not so much a despising of death as a want of regard for life that forms the characteristic feature. To this want of regard for life must be ascribed the great courage, supported by enormous bodily strength, exhibited by the Negroes, who allow themselves to be shot down by thousands in war with Europeans. Life has a value only when it has something valuable as its object.

Turning our attention in the next place to the category of *political constitution,* we shall see that the entire nature of this race is such as to preclude the existence of any such arrangement. The standpoint of humanity at this grade is mere sensuous volition with energy of will; since universal spiritual laws (for example, that of the morality of the Family) cannot be recognized here. Universality exists only as arbitrary subjective choice. The political bond can therefore not possess such a character as that free laws should unite the community. There is absolutely no bond, no restraint upon that arbitrary volition. Nothing but external force can hold the State together for a moment. A ruler stands at the head, for sensuous barbarism can only be restrained by despotic power. But since the subjects are of equally violent temper with their master, they keep him on the other hand within limits. Under the chief there are many other chiefs with whom the former, whom we will call the King, takes counsel, and whose consent he must seek to gain, if he wishes to undertake a war or impose a tax. In this relation he can exercise more or less authority, and by fraud or force can on occasion put this or that chieftain out of the way. Besides this the Kings have other specified prerogatives. Among the Ashantees the King inherits all the property left by his subjects at their death. In other places all unmarried women belong to the King, and whoever wishes a wife, must buy her from him. If the Negroes are discontented with their King they depose and kill him. In Dahomey, when they are thus displeased, the custom is to send parrots' eggs to the King, as a sign of dissatisfaction with his government. Sometimes also a deputation is sent, which intimates to him, that the burden of government must have been very troublesome to him, and that he had better rest a little. The King then thanks his subjects, goes into his apartments, and has himself strangled by the women. Tradition alleges that in former times a state composed of women made itself famous by its conquests: it was a state at whose head was a woman. She is said to have pounded her own son in a mortar, to have besmeared herself with the blood, and to have had the blood of pounded children constantly at hand. She is said to have driven away or put to death all the males, and commanded the death of all male children. These furies destroyed everything in the neighborhood, and were driven to constant plunderings, because they did not cultivate the land. Captives in war were taken as husbands: pregnant women had to betake themselves outside the encampment; and if they had born a son, put him out of the way. This infamous state, the report goes on to say, subsequently disappeared. Accompanying the King we constantly find in Negro States, the executioner, whose office is regarded as of the highest consideration, and by whose hands, the King, though he makes use of him for putting suspected persons to death, may himself suffer death, if the grandees desire it. Fanaticism, which, notwithstanding the yielding disposition of the Negro in other respects, can be excited, surpasses, when roused, all belief. An English traveller states that when a war is determined on in Ashantee, solemn ceremonies precede it: among other things the bones of the King's mother are laved with human blood. As a prelude to the war, the King ordains an onslaught upon his own metropolis, as if to excite the due degree of frenzy. The King sent word to the English Hutchinson: 'Christian, take care, and watch well over your family. The messenger of death has drawn his sword and will strike the neck of many Ashantees; when the drum sounds it is the death signal for multitudes. Come to the King, if you can, and fear nothing for yourself." The drum beat, and a terrible carnage was begun; all who came in the way of the frenzied Negroes in the streets were stabbed. On such occasions the King has all whom he suspects killed, and the deed then assumes the character of a sacred act. Every idea thrown into the mind of the Negro is caught up and realized with the whole energy of his will; but this realization involves a wholesale destruction. These people continue long at rest, but suddenly their passions ferment, and then they are quite beside themselves. The destruction which is the consequence of their excitement, is caused by the fact that it is no positive idea, no thought which produces these commotions; – a physical rather than a spiritual enthusiasm. In Dahomey, when the King dies, the bonds of society are loosed; in his palace begins indiscriminate havoc and disorganization. All the wives of the King (in Dahomey their number is exactly 3,333) are massacred, and through the whole town plunder and carnage run riot. The wives of the King regard this their death as a necessity; they go richly attired to meet it. The authorities have to hasten to proclaim the new governor, simply to put a stop to massacre.

From these various traits it is manifest that want of self-control distinguishes the character of the Negroes. This condition is capable of no development or culture, and as we see them at this day, such have they always been. The only essential connection that has existed and continued between the Negroes and the Europeans is that of slavery. In this the Negroes see nothing unbecoming them, and the English who have done most for abolishing the slave-trade and slavery, are treated by the Negroes themselves as enemies. For it is a point of first importance with the Kings to sell their captured enemies, or even their own subjects; and viewed in the light of such facts, we may conclude *slavery* to have been the occasion of the increase of human feeling among the Negroes. The doctrine which we deduce from this condition of slavery among the Negroes, and which constitutes the only side of the question that has an interest for our inquiry, is that which we deduce from the Idea: viz., that the "Natural condition" itself is one of absolute and thorough injustice – contravention of the Right and Just. Every intermediate grade between this and the realization of a rational State retains – as might be expected – elements and aspects of injustice; therefore we find slavery even in the Greek and Roman States, as we do serfdom down to the latest times. But thus existing in a State, slavery is itself a phase of advance from the merely isolated sensual existence – a phase of education – a mode of becoming participant in a higher morality and the culture connected with it. Slavery is in and for itself *injustice,* for the essence of humanity is *Freedom;* but for this man must be matured. The gradual abolition of slavery is therefore wiser and more equitable than its sudden removal.

At this point we leave Africa, not to mention it again. For it is no historical part of the World; it has no movement or development to exhibit. Historical movements in it – that is in its northern part – belong to the Asiatic or European World. Carthage displayed there an important transitionary phase of civilization; but, as a Phoenician colony, it belongs to Asia. Egypt will be considered in reference to the passage of the human mind from its Eastern to its Western phase, but it does not belong to the African Spirit. What we properly understand by Africa, is the Unhistorical, Undeveloped Spirit, still involved in the conditions of mere nature, and which had to be presented here only as on the threshold of the World's History. Having eliminated this introductory element, we find ourselves for the first time on the real theatre of History. It now only remains for us to give a prefatory sketch of the Geographical basis of the Asiatic and European world. *Asia* is, characteristically, the *Orient* quarter of the globe – the region of origination. It is indeed a Western world for

America; but as Europe presents on the whole, the centre and end of the old world, and is absolutely the *West – so* Asia is absolutely the *East.*

In Asia arose the Light of Spirit, and therefore the history of the World.

We must now consider the various localities of Asia. Its physical constitution presents direct antitheses, and the essential relation of these antitheses. Its various geographical principles are formations in themselves developed and perfected. First, the northern slope, Siberia, must be eliminated. This slope, from the Altai chain, with its fine streams, that pour their waters into the northern Ocean, does not at all concern us here; because the Northern Zone, as already stated, lies out of the pale of History. But the remainder includes three very interesting localities. The first is, as in Africa, a massive Upland, with a mountain girdle which contains the highest summits in the World. This Upland is bounded on the South and Southeast, by the Mus-Tag or Imaus, parallel to which, farther south, runs the Himalaya chain. Towards the East, a mountain chain running from South to North, parts off the basin of the Amur. On the North lie the Altai and Songarian mountains; in connection with the latter, in the Northwest the Musart and in the West the Belur Tag, which by the Hindoo Coosh chain are again united with the Mus-Tag.

This high mountain-girdle is broken through by streams, which are dammed up and form great valley plains. These, more or less inundated, present centres of excessive luxuriance and fertility, and are distinguished from the European river districts in their not forming, as those do, proper valleys with valleys branching out from them, but river-plains. Of this kind are – the Chinese Valley Plain, formed by the Hoang-Ho and Yang-tse-Kiang (the yellow and blue streams) – next that of India, formed by the Ganges; – less important is the Indus, which in the north, gives character to the Punjaub, and in the south flows through plains of sand. Farther on, the lands of the Tigris and Euphrates, which rise in Armenia and hold their course along the Persian mountains. The Caspian sea has similar river valleys; in the East those formed by the Oxus and Jaxartes (Gihon and Sihon) which pour their waters into the Sea of Aral; on the West those of the Cyrus and Araxes (Kur and Aras). – The Upland and the Plains must be distinguished from each other; the third element is their intermixture, which occurs in Hither [Anterior] Asia. To this belongs Arabia, the land of the Desert, the upland of plains, the empire of fanaticism. To this belong Syria and Asia Minor, connected with the sea, and having constant intercourse with Europe.

In regard to Asia the remark above offered respecting geographical differences is especially true; viz., that the rearing of cattle is the business of the Upland – agriculture and industrial pursuits that of the valley-plains – while commerce and navigation form the third and last item. Patriarchal independence is strictly bound up with the first condition of society; property and the relation of lord and serf with the second; civil freedom with the third. In the Upland, where the various kinds of cattle breeding, the rearing of horses, camels, and sheep, (not so much of oxen) deserve attention, we must also distinguish the calm *habitual* life of nomad tribes from the wild and restless character they display in their conquests. These people, without developing themselves in a really historical form, are swayed by a powerful impulse leading them to change their aspect as nations; and although *they* have not attained an historical character, the beginning of History may be traced to them. It must however be allowed that the peoples of the plains are more interesting. In agriculture itself is involved, *ipso facto,* the cessation of a roving life. It demands foresight and solicitude for the future: reflection on a general idea is thus awakened; and herein lies the principle of property and productive industry. China, India, Babylonia, have risen to the position of cultivated lands of this kind. But as the peoples that have occupied these lands have been shut up within themselves, and have not appropriated that element of civilization which the sea supplies, (or at any rate only at the commencement of their civilization) and as their navigation of it – to whatever extent it may have taken place – remained without influence on their culture – a relation to the rest of History could only exist in their case, through their being sought out, and their character investigated by others. The mountain-girdle of the upland, the upland itself, and the river-plains, characterize Asia physically and spiritually : but they themselves are not concretely, really, historical elements. The opposition between the extremes is simply recognized, not harmonized; a firm settlement in the fertile plains is for the mobile, restless, roving, condition of the mountain and Upland races, nothing more than a constant object of endeavor. Physical features distinct in the sphere of nature, assume an essential historical relation. – Anterior Asia has both elements in one, and has, consequently, a relation to Europe; for what is most remarkable in it, this land has not kept for itself, but sent over to Europe. It presents the origination of all religious and political principles, but Europe has been the scene of their development.

Europe, to which we now come, has not the physical varieties which we noticed in Asia and Africa. The European character involves the disappearance of the contrast exhibited by earlier varieties, or at least a modification of it; so that we have the milder qualities of a transition state. We have in Europe no uplands immediately contrasted with plains. The three sections of Europe require therefore a different basis of classification. The first part is Southern Europe – looking towards the Mediterranean. North of the Pyrenees, mountain-chains run through France, connected with the Alps that separate and cut off Italy from France and Germany. Greece also belongs to this part of Europe. Greece and Italy long presented the theatre of the World's History; and while the middle and north of Europe were uncultivated, the World-Spirit found its home here. The second portion is the heart of Europe, which Caesar opened when conquering Gaul. This achievement was one of manhood on the part of the *Roman* General, and more productive than that youthful one of Alexander, who undertook to exalt the East to a participation in Greek life; and whose work, though in its purport the noblest and fairest for the imagination, soon vanished, as a mere Ideal, in the sequel. – In this centre of Europe, France, Germany, and England are the principal countries.

Lastly, the third part consists of the north-eastern States of Europe – Poland, Russia, and the Slavonic Kingdoms. They come only late into the series of historical States, and form and perpetuate the connection with Asia. In contrast with the physical peculiarities of the earlier divisions, these are, as already noticed, not present in a remarkable degree, but counterbalance each other.

CLASSIFICATION OF HISTORIC DATA

In the geographical survey, the course of the World's History has been marked out in its general features. The *Sun* – the Light – rises in the East. Light is a simply self-involved existence; but though possessing thus in itself universality, it exists at the same time as an individuality in the Sun. Imagination has often pictured to itself the emotions of a blind man suddenly becoming possessed of sight, beholding the bright glimmering of the dawn, the growing light, and the flaming glory of the ascending Sun. The boundless forgetfulness of his individuality in this pure splendor, is his first feeling – utter astonishment. But when the Sun is risen, this astonishment is diminished; objects around are perceived, and from them the individual proceeds to the contemplation of his own inner being, and thereby the advance is made to the perception of the relation between the two. Then inactive contemplation is quitted for activity; by the close of day man has erected a building constructed from his own inner Sun; and when in the evening he contemplates this, he esteems it more highly than the original external Sun. For now he stands in a *conscious relation* to his Spirit, and therefore a *free* relation. If we hold this image fast in mind, we shall find it symbolizing the course of History, the great Day's work of Spirit. The History of the World travels from East to West, for Europe is absolutely the end of History, Asia the beginning. The History of the World has an East κατ ξοχην; (the term East in itself is entirely relative), for although the Earth forms a sphere, History performs no circle round it, but has on the contrary a determinate East, viz., Asia. Here rises the outward physical Sun, and in the West it sinks down: here consentaneously rises the Sun of self-consciousness, which diffuses a nobler brilliance. The History of the World is the discipline of the uncontrolled natural will, bringing it into obedience to a Universal principle and conferring subjective freedom. The East knew and to the present day knows only that *One* is Free; the

Greek and Roman world, that *some* are free; the German World knows that *All* are free. The first political form therefore which we observe in History, is *Despotism,* the second *Democracy* and *Aristocracy,* the third *Monarchy.*

To understand this division we must remark that as the State is the universal spiritual life, to which individuals by birth sustain a relation of confidence and habit, and in which they have their existence and reality – the first question is, whether their actual life is an unreflecting use and habit combining them in this unity, or whether its constituent individuals are reflective and personal beings having a properly subjective and independent existence. In view of this, *substantial* [objective] freedom must be distinguished from *subjective* freedom. Substantial freedom is the abstract undeveloped Reason implicit in volition, proceeding to develop itself in the State. But in this phase of Reason there is still wanting personal insight and will, that is, subjective freedom; which is realized only in the Individual, and which constitutes the reflection of the Individual in his own conscience.[7] Where there is merely substantial freedom, commands and laws are regarded as something fixed and abstract, to which the subject holds himself in absolute servitude. These laws need not concur with the desire of the individual, and the subjects are consequently like children, who obey their parents without will or insight of their own. But as subjective freedom arises, and man descends from the contemplation of external reality into his own soul, the contrast suggested by reflection arises, involving the Negation of Reality. The drawing back from the actual world forms *ipso facto* an antithesis, of which one side is the absolute Being, – the Divine – the other the human subject as an individual. In that immediate, unreflected consciousness which characterizes the East, these two are not yet distinguished. The substantial world is distinct from the individual, but the antithesis has not yet created a schism between (absolute and subjective) Spirit.

The first phase – that with which we have to begin – is the *East.* Unreflected consciousness – substantial, objective, spiritual existence – forms the basis; to which the subjective will first sustains a relation in the form of faith, confidence, obedience. In the political life of the East we find a realized rational freedom, developing itself without advancing to

116

subjective freedom. It is the childhood of History. Substantial forms constitute the gorgeous edifices of Oriental *Empires* in which we find all rational ordinances and arrangements, but in such a way, that individuals remain as mere accidents. These revolve round a centre, round the sovereign, who, as patriarch – not as despot in the sense of the *Roman* Imperial Constitution – stands at the head. For he has to enforce the moral and substantial: he has to uphold those essential ordinances which are already established ; so that what among us belongs entirely to subjective freedom, here proceeds from the entire and general body of the State. The glory of Oriental conception is the One Individual as that substantial being to which all belongs, so that no other individual has a separate existence, or mirrors himself in his subjective freedom. All the riches of imagination and Nature are appropriated to that dominant existence in which subjective freedom is essentially merged; the latter looks for its dignity *not* in itself, but in that absolute object. All the elements of a complete State – even subjectivity – may be found there, but not yet harmonized with the grand substantial being. For outside the One Power – before which nothing can maintain an independent existence – there is only revolting caprice, which, beyond the limits of the central power, roves at will without purpose or result. Accordingly we find the wild hordes breaking out from the Upland – falling upon the countries in question, and laying them waste, or settling down in them, and giving up their wild life; but in all cases resultlessly lost in the central substance. This phase of Substantiality, since it has not taken up its antithesis into itself and overcome it, directly divides itself into two elements. On the one side we see duration, stability – Empires belonging to mere space, as it were (as distinguished from Time) – unhistorical History; – as for example, in China, the State based on the Family relation; – a paternal Government, which holds together the constitution by its provident care, its admonitions, retributive or rather disciplinary inflictions; – a prosaic Empire, because the antithesis of Form, viz., Infinity, Ideality, has not yet asserted itself. On the other side, the Form of Tame stands contrasted with this spatial stability. The States in question, without undergoing any change in themselves, or in the principle of their existence, are constantly changing their position towards each other. They are in ceaseless conflict, which brings on. rapid destruction. The opposing principle of individuality enters into these conflicting

117

relations; but it is itself as yet only unconscious, merely natural Universality – Light, which is not yet the light of the personal soul. This History, too (*i.e.,* of the struggles before-mentioned) is, for the most part, really *unhis-torical,* for it is only the repetition of the same majestic ruin. The new element, which in the shape of bravery, prowess, magnanimity, occupies the place of the previous despotic pomp, goes through the same circle of decline and subsidence. This subsidence is therefore not really such, for through all this restless change no advance is made. History passes at this point – and only outwardly, *i.e.,* without connection with the previous phase – to Central Asia.

Continuing the comparison with the ages of the individual man, this would be the boyhood of History, no longer manifesting the repose and trustingness of the child, but boisterous and turbulent. The Greek World may then be compared with the period of adolescence, for here we have individualities forming themselves. This is the *second* main principle in human History. Morality is, as in Asia, a principle ; but it is morality impressed on individuality, and consequently denoting the free volition of Individuals. Here, then, is the Union of the Moral with the subjective Will, or the Kingdom of *Beautiful Freedom,* for the Idea is united with a plastic form. It is not yet regarded abstractedly, but immediately bound up with the Real, as in a beautiful work of Art; the Sensuous bears the stamp and expression of the Spiritual. This Kingdom is consequently true Harmony; the world of the most charming, but perishable or quickly passing bloom: it is the natural, unreflecting observance of what is *becoming* – not yet true *Morality.* The individual will of the Subject adopts unreflectingly the conduct and habit prescribed by Justice and the Laws. The Individual is therefore in unconscious unity with the Idea – the social weal. That which in the East is divided into two extremes – the substantial as such, and the individuality absorbed in it – meets here. But these distinct principles are only *immediately* in unity, and consequently involve the highest degree of contradiction; for this aesthetic Morality has not yet passed through the struggle of subjective freedom, in its second birth, its *palingenesis,* it is not yet purified to the standard of the free subjectivity that is the essence of true morality.

The third phase is the realm of abstract Universality (in which the Social aim absorbs all individual aims) : it is the *Roman State,* the severe labors

118

of the *Manhood* of History. For true manhood acts neither in accordance with the caprice of a despot, nor in obedience to a graceful caprice of its own; but works for a general aim, one in which the individual perishes and realizes his own private object only in that general aim. The State begins to have an abstract existence, and to develop itself for a definite object, in accomplishing which its members have indeed a share, but not a complete and concrete one [calling their whole being into play]. Free *individuals* are sacrificed to the severe demands of the *National* objects, to which they must surrender themselves in this service of abstract generalization. The Roman State is not a repetition of such a State of Individuals as the Athenian Polis was. The geniality and joy of soul that existed there have given place to harsh and rigorous toil. The interest of History is detached from individuals, but these gain for themselves abstract, formal Universality. The Universal subjugates the individuals; they have to merge their own interests in it; but in return the abstraction which they themselves embody – that is to say, their personality – is recognized: in their individual capacity they become persons with definite rights as such. In the same sense as individuals may be said to be incorporated in the abstract idea of Person, *National Individualities* (those of the Roman Provinces) have also to experience this fate: in this form of Universality their concrete forms are crushed, and incorporated with it as a homogeneous and indifferent mass. Rome becomes a Pantheon of all deities, and of all Spiritual existence, but these divinities and this Spirit do not retain their proper vitality. – The development of the State in question proceeds in two directions. On the one hand, as based on reflection – abstract Universality – it has the express outspoken antithesis in itself: it therefore essentially involves in itself the struggle which that antithesis supposes; with the necessary issue, that individual caprice – the purely contingent and thoroughly worldly power of *one despot* – gets the better of that abstract universal principle. At the very outset we have the antithesis between the Aim of the State as the abstract universal principle on the one hand, and the abstract personality of the individual on the other hand. But when subsequently, in the historical development, individuality gains the ascendant, and the breaking up of the community into its component atoms can only be restrained by external compulsion, then the subjective might of *individual despotism* comes forward to play its part, as if summoned to fulfil this task. For the

119

mere abstract compliance with Law implies on the part of the subject of law the supposition that he has not attained to selforganization and self-control ; and this principle of obedience, instead of being hearty and voluntary, has for its motive and ruling power only the arbitrary and contingent disposition of the individual; so that the latter is led to seek consolation for the loss of his freedom in exercising and developing his private right. This is the purely *worldly* harmonization of the antithesis. But in the next place, the pain inflicted by Despotism begins to be felt, and Spirit driven back into its utmost depths, leaves the godless world, seeks for a harmony in itself, and begins now an inner life – a complete concrete subjectivity, which possesses at the same time a substantiality that is not grounded in mere external existence. Within the soul therefore arises the *Spiritual* pacification of the struggle, in the fact that the individual personality, instead of following its own capricious choice, is purified and elevated into universality; – a subjectivity that of its own free will adopts principles tending to the good of all – reaches, in fact, a divine personality. To that worldly empire, this Spiritual one wears a predominant aspect of opposition, as the empire of a subjectivity that has attained to the knowledge of itself – itself in its essential nature – the Empire of Spirit in its full sense.

The *German* world appears at this point of development – the fourth phase of World-History. This would answer in the comparison with the periods of human life to its *Old Age.* The Old Age of *Nature* is weakness; but that of *Spirit* is its perfect maturity and *strength,* in which it returns to unity with itself, but in its fully developed character as *Spirit.* – This fourth phase begins with the Reconciliation presented in Christianity; but only in the germ, without national or political development. We must therefore regard it as commencing rather with the enormous contrast between the spiritual, religious principle, and the barbarian Real World. For Spirit as the consciousness of an inner World is, at the commencement, itself still in an abstract form. All that is *secular* is consequently given over to rudeness and capricious violence. The *Mohammedan* principle – the enlightenment of the Oriental World – is the first to contravene this barbarism and caprice. We find it developing itself later and more rapidly than Christianity; for the latter needed eight centuries to grow up into a political form. But that principle of the

German World which we are now discussing, attained concrete reality only in the history of the German Nations. The contrast of the Spiritual principle animating the *Ecclesiastical* State, with the rough and wild barbarism of the *Secular* State, is here likewise present. The Secular *ought* to be in harmony with the Spiritual principle, but we find nothing more than the *recognition* of that obligation. The Secular power forsaken by the Spirit, must in the first instance vanish in presence of the Ecclesiastical (as representative of Spirit) ; but while this latter degrades itself to mere secularity, it loses its influence with the loss of its proper character and vocation. From this corruption of the Ecclesiastical element – that is, of the Church – results the higher form of rational thought. Spirit once more driven back upon itself, produces its work in an intellectual shape, and becomes capable of realizing the Ideal of Reason from the Secular principle alone. Thus it happens, that in virtue of elements of Universality, which have the principle of Spirit as their basis, the empire of Thought is established actually and concretely. The antithesis of Church and State vanishes. The Spiritual becomes reconnected with the Secular, and develops this latter as an independently organic existence. The State no longer occupies a position of real inferiority to the Church, and is no longer subordinate to it. The latter asserts no prerogative, and the Spiritual is no longer an element foreign to the State. Freedom has found the means of realizing its Ideal – its true existence. This is the ultimate result which the process of History is intended to accomplish, and we have to traverse in detail the long track which has been thus cursorily traced out. Yet length of Time is something entirely relative, and the element of Spirit is Eternity. Duration, properly speaking, cannot be said to belong to it.

NOTES

1. Mr. G. H. Lewes, in his *Biographical History of Philosophy*, Vol. IV, Ed. 1841.

2. I cannot mention any work that will serve as a compendium of the course, but I may remark that in my "Outlines of the Philosophy of Law," §§341-360, I have already given a definition of such a Universal History as it is proposed to develop, and a syllabus of the chief elements or periods into which it naturally divides itself.

3. Fr. von Schlegel, "Philosophy of History," p. 91, Bohn's Standard Library.

4. We have to thank this interest for many valuable discoveries in Oriental literature, and for a renewed study of treasures previously known, in the department of ancient Asiatic Culture, Mythology, Religions, and History. In Catholic countries, where a refined literary taste prevails, Governments have yielded to the requirements of speculative inquiry, and have felt the necessity of allying themselves with learning and philosophy. Eloquently and impressively has the Abbé Lamennais reckoned it among the criteria of the true religion, that it must be the universal – that is, catholic – and the oldest in date; and the Congregation has labored zealously and diligently in France towards rendering such assertions no longer mere pulpit tirades and authoritative dicta, such as were deemed sufficient formerly. The religion of Buddha – a godman – which has prevailed to such an enormous extent, has especially attracted attention. The Indian Timûrtis, as also the Chinese abstraction of the Trinity, has furnished clearer evidence in point of subject matter. The savants, M. Abel Remusat and M. Saint Martin, on the one hand, have undertaken the most meritorious investigations in the Chinese literature, with a view to make this also a base of operations for researches in the Mongolian and, if such were possible, in the Thibetan; on the other hand, Baron von Eckstein – in his way (*i.e.,* adopting from Germany superficial physical conceptions and mannerisms, in the style of Fr. v. Schlegel, though with more geniality than the latter) in his periodical, "Le Catholique" – has furthered the cause of that primitive Catholicism generally, and in particular has gained for the savans of the

Congregation the support of the Government; so that it has even set on foot expeditions to the East, in order to discover there treasures still concealed; (from which further disclosures have been anticipated, respecting profound theological questions, particularly on the higher antiquity and sources of Buddhism), and with a view to promote the interests of Catholicism by this circuitous but scientifically interesting method.

5. German, "Geschichte" from "Geschehen," to happen. – ED. *Vide* Hegel's "Vorlesungen über die Philosophie der Religion," I. 284 and 289. 2d Ed.

6. The essence of Spirit is self-determination or "Freedom." Where Spirit has attained mature growth, as in the man who acknowledges the absolute validity of the dictates of Conscience, the Individual is "a law to himself," and this Freedom is "realized." But in lower stages of morality and civilization, he *unconsciously projects* this legislative principle into some "governing power" (one or several), and obeys it as if it were an alien, extraneous force, not the voice of that Spirit of which he himself (though at this stage imperfectly) is an embodiment. The Philosophy of History exhibits the successive stages by which he reaches the consciousness, that it is *his own inmost being* that thus governs him – *i.e.,* a consciousness of self-determination or "Freedom." – ED.

7. It is evident that the term "*moral* standpoint" is used here in the strict sense in which Hegel has defined it, in his "Philosophy of Law," as that of the self-determination of subjectivity, *free conviction* of the Good. The reader, therefore, should not misunderstand the use that continues to be made of the terms, morality, moral government, etc., in reference to the Chinese; as they denote morality only in the loose and ordinary meaning of the word – precepts or commands given with a view to producing good behavior – without bringing into relief the element of internal conviction. – ED.

3103508

Made in the USA